Joyce Appleby on *Thomas Jefferson*

Louis Auchincloss on *Theodore Roosevelt*

Jean H. Baker on *James Buchanan*

John M. Blum on *William Howard Taft*

H. W. Brands on *Woodrow Wilson*

Douglas Brinkley on *Gerald R. Ford*

Josiah Bunting III on *Ulysses S. Grant*

James MacGregor Burns and Susan Dunn on *George Washington*

Charles W. Calhoun on *Benjamin Harrison*

Robert Dallek on *Harry S. Truman*

John W. Dean on *Warren G. Harding*

John Patrick Diggins on *John Adams*

E. L. Doctorow on *Abraham Lincoln*

Annette Gordon-Reed on *Andrew Johnson*

Henry F. Graff on *Grover Cleveland*

Gary Hart on *James Monroe*

Hendrik Hertzberg on *Jimmy Carter*

Roy Jenkins on *Franklin Delano Roosevelt*

Zachary Karabell on *Chester Alan Arthur*

William E. Leuchtenburg on *Herbert Hoover*

Timothy Naftali on *George Bush*

Kevin Phillips on *William McKinley*

Robert V. Remini on *John Quincy Adams*

John Seigenthaler on *James K. Polk*

Hans L. Trefousse on *Rutherford B. Hayes*

Tom Wicker on *Dwight D. Eisenhower*

Ted Widmer on *Martin Van Buren*

Sean Wilentz on *Andrew Jackson*

Garry Wills on *James Madison*

Ulysses S. Grant

Josiah Bunting III

Ulysses S. Grant

THE AMERICAN PRESIDENTS

ARTHUR M. SCHLESINGER, JR., GENERAL EDITOR

Times Books

HENRY HOLT AND COMPANY, NEW YORK

Times Books
Henry Holt and Company, LLC
Publishers since 1866
115 West 18th Street
New York, New York 10011

Henry Holt® is a registered trademark of Henry Holt and Company, LLC.

Copyright © 2004 by Josiah Bunting III
All rights reserved.
Distributed in Canada by H. B. Fenn and Company Ltd.

LIBRARY OF CONGRESS CATALOGING-IN-PUBLICATION DATA
Bunting, Josiah, 1939–
    Ulysses S. Grant / Josiah Bunting III.—1st ed.
        p.   cm.—(The American presidents series)
    Includes bibliographical references and index.
    ISBN 0-8050-6949-6
    1. Grant, Ulysses S. (Ulysses Simpson), 1822–1885.   2. Presidents—United
States—Biography.   3. United States—Politics and government—1869–1877.
I. Title.   II. American presidents series (Times Books (Firm))
E672.B93 2004
973.8'2'092—dc22
[B]   2004047889

First Edition 2004

Printed in the United States of America
3   5   7   9   10   8   6   4

To Howard Cushing

It is not easy to discern the motives of any action by any person, especially since our reasons for doing something are often hidden even to ourselves. . . . Those who do not explain themselves often find themselves explained by others.

MICHAEL B. BECKERMAN,
New Worlds of Dvorak

Contents

Editor's Note

THE AMERICAN PRESIDENCY

The president is the central player in the American political order. That would seem to contradict the intentions of the Founding Fathers. Remembering the horrid example of the British monarchy, they invented a separation of powers in order, as Justice Brandeis later put it, "to preclude the exercise of arbitrary power." Accordingly, they divided the government into three allegedly equal and coordinate branches—the executive, the legislative, and the judiciary.

But a system based on the tripartite separation of powers has an inherent tendency toward inertia and stalemate. One of the three branches must take the initiative if the system is to move. The executive branch alone is structurally capable of taking that initiative. The Founders must have sensed this when they accepted Alexander Hamilton's proposition in the Seventieth Federalist that "energy in the executive is a leading character in the definition of good government." They thus envisaged a strong president—but within an equally strong system of constitutional accountability. (The term *imperial presidency* arose in the 1970s to describe the situation when the balance between power and accountability is upset in favor of the executive.)

The American system of self-government thus comes to focus in the presidency—"the vital place of action in the system," as Woodrow

Wilson put it. Henry Adams, himself the great-grandson and grandson of presidents as well as the most brilliant of American historians, said that the American president "resembles the commander of a ship at sea. He must have a helm to grasp, a course to steer, a port to seek." The men in the White House (thus far only men, alas) in steering their chosen courses have shaped our destiny as a nation.

Biography offers an easy education in American history, rendering the past more human, more vivid, more intimate, more accessible, more connected to ourselves. Biography reminds us that presidents are not supermen. They are human beings too, worrying about decisions, attending to wives and children, juggling balls in the air, and putting on their pants one leg at a time. Indeed, as Emerson contended, "There is properly no history; only biography."

Presidents serve us as inspirations, and they also serve us as warnings. They provide bad examples as well as good. The nation, the Supreme Court has said, has "no right to expect that it will always have wise and humane rulers, sincerely attached to the principles of the Constitution. Wicked men, ambitious of power, with hatred of liberty and contempt of law, may fill the place once occupied by Washington and Lincoln."

The men in the White House express the ideals and the values, the frailties and the flaws of the voters who send them there. It is altogether natural that we should want to know more about the virtues and the vices of the fellows we have elected to govern us. As we know more about them, we will know more about ourselves. The French political philosopher Joseph de Maistre said, "Every nation has the government it deserves."

At the start of the twenty-first century, forty-two men have made it to the oval office. (George W. Bush is counted our forty-third president because Grover Cleveland, who served nonconsecutive terms, is counted twice.) Of the parade of presidents, a dozen or so lead the polls periodically conducted by historians and political scientists. What makes a great president?

Great presidents possess, or are possessed by, a vision of an ideal America. Their passion, as they grasp the helm, is to set the ship of state on the right course toward the port they seek. Great presidents also have a deep psychic connection with the needs, anxieties, dreams of people. "I do not believe," said Wilson, "that any man can lead who does not act . . . under the impulse of a profound sympathy with those whom he leads—a sympathy which is insight—an insight which is of the heart rather than of the intellect."

"All of our great presidents," said Franklin D. Roosevelt, "were leaders of thought at a time when certain ideas in the life of the nation had to be clarified." So Washington incarnated the idea of federal union, Jefferson and Jackson the idea of democracy, Lincoln union and freedom, Cleveland rugged honesty. Theodore Roosevelt and Wilson, said FDR, were both "moral leaders, each in his own way and his own time, who used the presidency as a pulpit."

To succeed, presidents must not only have a port to seek but they must convince Congress and the electorate that it is a port worth seeking. Politics in a democracy is ultimately an educational process, an adventure in persuasion and consent. Every president stands in Theodore Roosevelt's bully pulpit.

The greatest presidents in the scholars' rankings, Washington, Lincoln, and Franklin Roosevelt, were leaders who confronted and overcame the republic's greatest crises. Crisis widens presidential opportunities for bold and imaginative action. But it does not guarantee presidential greatness. The crisis of secession did not spur Buchanan or the crisis of depression spur Hoover to creative leadership. Their inadequacies in the face of crisis allowed Lincoln and the second Roosevelt to show the difference individuals make to history. Still, even in the absence of first-order crisis, forceful and persuasive presidents—Jefferson, Jackson, Theodore Roosevelt, Ronald Reagan—are able to impose their own priorities on the country.

The diverse drama of the presidency offers a fascinating set of tales. Biographies of American presidents constitute a chronicle of wisdom and folly, nobility and pettiness, courage and cunning, forthrightness and deceit, quarrel and consensus. The turmoil perennially swirling around the White House illuminates the heart of the American democracy.

It is the aim of the American Presidents series to present the grand panorama of our chief executives in volumes compact enough for the busy reader, lucid enough for the student, authoritative enough for the scholar. Each volume offers a distillation of character and career. I hope that these lives will give readers some understanding of the pitfalls and potentialities of the presidency and also of the responsibilities of citizenship. Truman's famous sign—"The buck stops here"—tells only half the story. Citizens cannot escape the ultimate responsibility. It is in the voting booth, not on the presidential desk, that the buck finally stops.

—Arthur M. Schlesinger, Jr.

Ulysses S. Grant

Introduction:
The Problem of Grant

From the end of the Civil War and the assassination of Abraham Lincoln five days later, and until his own death in 1885, Ulysses S. Grant was first in the hearts of his countrymen. They saluted him as a savior of the Union. He was the most famous and most carefully scrutinized American. Elected president by a modest majority in 1868, he was reelected four years later by an overwhelming majority; and although his second term was full of contention, disappointment, and "scandal," he retained a certain hold on citizens' affections and the full measure of their gratitude—a gratitude that largely transcended their political judgment of his service. His decision not to seek a third term in 1876 was seen as honorable and forbearing. After fifteen years' service as general and president, he had earned his rest.

Grant's conduct as an ex-president (during the presidencies of Rutherford B. Hayes, James A. Garfield, and Chester Alan Arthur) served to make him more popular; he was beloved. His heroic fight against a terrible cancer, the continuing magnanimity of his judgments about men formerly his enemies, his survival with grace through a financial ruin not of his own making—such things commended him to all. His funeral in New York City, in which southern contingents marched proudly near the front of the procession, was an occasion for an overwhelming outpouring of public gratitude, mourning, affection. A giant had left the country, and the nation knew it.

For most of the time of his public florescence (1862–85), however, no one really knew quite what to make of Ulysses S. Grant. He
was a profound puzzle to his own generation; the character of his
gifts resisted and frustrated their powers of analysis; his taciturnity
(*taciturn* and *imperturbable* are among the most common adjectives
in the lexicon of Grant commentary) denied them his own views
and justifications for what he had done. Grant was rarely an
explainer or justifier. In politics as in war, he addressed his problems, discharged his mission, and moved on. Like the Julius Caesar
of the war commentaries (to which Grant's own *Memoirs* would
be compared), he moved irresistibly forward: "These things having
been accomplished, next Caesar turned his attention to . . ." Grant
was, of course, a writer of famously pellucid military orders, and he
was a man capable of an almost inhuman disinterestedness in reaching judgments about strategy: he saw things bluntly and directly. Of
his possession of that rare combination of those qualities of character and mind that make for a great commander, there is and was no
question. But the nature of that combination seems to have eluded
people of his own time who tried to explain it, just as it has, until
fairly recently, eluded biographers and historians who have tried (as
each generation must) to explain him.

There are several related issues. Grant was the only American
president to serve two complete and consecutive terms between
Andrew Jackson and Woodrow Wilson, and as president he was
bequeathed heavier and less tractable burdens than any other president in our history, save only two. The transformation of Great
Commander into President/Politician has been as difficult for historians to grasp as it must surely have been for the subject of their
studies—although Grant never let on that he gave it much thought.
He has been an enigma not only to Grant biographers but also to
generations of historical generalists and scholars, their difficulty in
assessment betrayed by their inability to write about him with anything approaching the objectivity and disinterestedness he both
prized and represented. Of no president are biases in judgment less
well disguised than in those that inform opinions about Ulysses
Grant. There is much acidulous curling of the lip in depictions and

opinions and judgments about him, an irremediable condescension stamped, it sometimes seems, on every page—even in the tartly acute, often funny chapters of the only single-volume major history of the Grant presidency: William Hesseltine's *Ulysses Grant*, now sixty-nine years old.

It is as though these writers can no more escape the clichés of the Grant Myth than the popular culture can, the popular culture in which he lives on as a shadowed icon, great but not good, above all opaque; even when he looks at the camera dead-on (the Cold Harbor photograph everyone knows, the one in front of the tent), there is an unfathomable opacity to him: an impenetrability that almost seems to dare people to impute things to him. He won us the war; he helped save the Plains Indians; he was the steady if tormented guarantor of Reconstruction (at least while he was president the black people had a chance); he evinced calm bravery in vetoing the inflation bill of 1874 (in the face of overwhelming political pressure to the contrary)—these are remarkable things he did. But the counts against him remain, sullen and immovable: *drunk, butcher, scandalmonger.* A crude sort of man, perhaps of the type we need to run a war, and, sometimes, to run the country, but these things do not entitle him to fair assessment, not with other things we know.

Under these vaguely recollected facts float a few others in mitigation: Wasn't he kind to Robert E. Lee at Appomattox (even though he wore a soiled uniform)? Didn't he write a great book, some kind of memoir, something to do with Mark Twain, that made his family enough money to live on, after he had died from cancer, up in the Adirondacks? The anecdotes that sustain these cameos seem preserved under a dusty lacquer: wasn't it Lincoln who said something about getting the other generals some of Grant's brand of whiskey, so that they too could win battles instead of talking about what they needed to win battles?

And didn't his huge battered columns, taking a sharp turn to the south in the Virginia Wilderness, after taking unspeakable losses, didn't they cheer in flat-out amazement that their chief was pushing them toward, not away from, the enemy who had whipped every other Yankee bandbox general sent after them? This was in the spring of 1864, when the word *butcher* began to be heard, when General Grant promised "to fight it out on this line if it takes all summer." The crude silent soldier who sat whittling in a clearing while reports of desperate casualties flowed in like a bloody tide. And, finally, for the minority of Americans who even remember that Ulysses Grant was president as well as general, did he not (in a phrase so worn it might almost be the start of an epithet) preside over the most corrupt administration in American history? This is why he must be last in all the rankings . . . et cetera.

Ulysses Grant has not been the kind of historical personage whom people who write history are likely to view with unprejudiced eyes. And there is another family of Grant anecdotes, received information, which present him as permanently in rebellion against, precisely, those things that historians (intellectuals, educated in the humane letters, reluctant to praise military men other than George C. Marshall or Colin Powell) believe or want to believe; after all, is not history written in order to equip rising generations with the knowledge, the "diagnostic ability," that will serve to immunize them against making the mistakes earlier generations have made? Invariably they take Grant to be anti-intellectual; pre-intellectual, Henry Adams would say—the same Henry Adams who wrote that to evolve from Alexander the Great to George Washington to Ulysses S. Grant was to disprove Darwin. They have tended to come at him with that bias. They, too, vaguely recollect Grant's comment about Venice: a nice city, if they'd drain the streets; and when you get him to Rome, take him to see the equestrian statue of Marcus Aurelius: he'll like the horse.

A clue to the Problem of Grant—the problem being that he has only rarely, and only recently, been fairly judged as President, not General, Grant—lies in the title of John Russell Young's wonderful portrait of the ex-president, *Around the World with General Grant*. Young was a *New York Herald* writer assigned to accompany the Grants on their trip around the world—a journey that would last two years and four months—and to file stories about their visits and meetings and expeditions abroad. When the party left Philadelphia in May 1877 (Young not yet with them), Grant's friend and confidant William Tecumseh Sherman offered the farewell toast. He reminded the guests that the man to whom they were saying good-bye was not President Grant but General Grant—the General Grant who, in the darkest days of the war, at Fort Donelson, had gained for the Union its first serious victory and brought it off in the finest style, telling his opponent (as it happened, a dear and lifelong friend): "No terms except complete and unconditional surrender can be accepted. I propose to move upon your works."

All during the long journey, wherever he was received, however carefully protocol labored to receive him as a "former sovereign," however exalted his former station, it was as *General* Grant that he was greeted and honored.

This is still how Grant is remembered: as a general, not a president, and it explains in part the condescension—there is no better word for it—with which pundits and historians have tended to write of him. There may be strength in his soul, but no fineness in it, no grace; little culture, small learning (none of it used to advantage in the regular uses of political intercourse), meager evidence of the capacity to learn and to reflect; no felt obligation to explain himself; no evidence of self-doubt. Generations of Grant scholars, too, have brought to their consideration of his presidency—of his whole career—the absorbing interests of their own times. By the turn of the century, and for the next fifty years, an unconscious racism inflected their judgments: black Americans, recently made free, had nothing of the training or predisposition (i.e., capacity) to undertake to govern themselves; Reconstruction, under Grant, was misjudged; and with Hayes came peace, in 1877, because Hayes understood that the states themselves could best deal with their—colored—problems. Grant, fully in the camp of the radical Republicans by the time he took office as president, ready to enforce bayonet rule by federal troops to "put down" troubles, was culpable in the execution of a vast misunderstanding of what was really needed in the South.

The Great War, 1914–18, and the slaughter that distinguished this most colossal barbarism in the history of the world, and the campaigns and battles on the western front, brought Grant the Butcher to the fore again: it forced consideration less of the achievements and terms of Appomattox than of the sixty-five thousand casualties in five weeks' fighting in the spring of 1864—in Virginia alone. And in the aftermath of the Harding presidency the scandals of Grant's own administration exerted a renewed fascination.

Historians writing in more recent years—Brooks Simpson, Jean Edward Smith, Frank Scaturro—have reversed the trend and tendency. They are getting beyond and beneath the clichés, and what Scaturro calls "literary" prejudices, the ungovernable indulgence in a weird kind of class depredation: the distaste of the well bred and educated for the provincial and, somehow, crude Ulysses. Above all they are reminding our contemporaries and a rising generation of the nature of the mission, and its monumental challenge, to which Grant, elected in 1868, was then committed. Simpson quotes a contemporary *Edinburgh Review* assessment: "To bind up the wounds left by the war, to restore concord to the still distracted Union, to ensure real freedom to the Southern Negro, and full justice to the southern white; these are indeed tasks which might tax the powers of Washington himself or a greater than Washington, if such a man is to be found."

The silent serenity in which Ulysses Grant seemed to move through life, whether the consequence of granitic self-command or physical disposition or long training in hard schools of disappointment, disregard, even failure, puzzled and fascinated his friends. It has guaranteed his friends and adversaries, contemporaries or members of generations a century later, would fill up the voids with their own imputations of what led and moved him to action. Sigmund Freud credited one of his teachers with a degree of simple common sense so great that it must be said to border on genius; common sense, judgment, intuition—such things cannot always be dissected. Instead, their consequences should be judged. By this criterion the Grant presidency, so far from being one of the nation's worst, may yet be seen as among its best.

He does remain a mystery, and that is the Problem of Grant. Children say much more than they know when they idly ask: Who is buried in Grant's tomb?

1

A Son of the West

For most of his life Ulysses S. Grant thought of himself as a westerner. He was a child of the great Valley of Democracy, born on April 27, 1822, a hundred yards from the north bank of the Ohio. The country thereabouts was less than a generation removed from raw frontier, Ohio having achieved statehood only nineteen years earlier, and the village of Point Pleasant, some twenty-five miles southeast of Cincinnati, was but a tiny huddle of cabins and rude frame houses. Ohio was the easternmost of the states being carved from the old Northwest Territory, but to New England and New York, to the original states of the Atlantic seaboard, it seemed still a remote West: raw and bountiful, unfettered, rich in possibility.

Forty years later, in 1862, it was as a western general that Grant achieved the sudden celebrity that seems peculiarly American, after his victory and successful demand for an unconditional surrender at Fort Donelson—a Union triumph that thrilled the country and resuscitated its hopes and confidence; and, just two years after that, it was as the famous leader of the western armies that he was selected to command all Union forces. He was "brought east." The small vignette of Grant's arrival in the grand lobby of Willard's Hotel in Washington, in March 1864, is an enduring cameo of American popular history: the most famous man in the country, next to Abraham Lincoln himself, signing the register as "U.S. Grant and son, Galena, Ill.," a traveler so small and dusty that the clerk did not recognize him; an unpretentious guest who could not, it appeared, have cared less. No doubt, too, the instinctive rapport between Abraham Lincoln and his new lieutenant general owed much to their common heritage as westerners—as James Russell Lowell said of Lincoln, "out of the very earth, unancestried, unprivileged, unknown"—and was demonstrated most powerfully in their common understanding of the needs of the South in the days just before, and just after, Appomattox.

Grant, it is true, was "ancestried" in a way that Lincoln was not. It was known that Matthew Grant had landed in Massachusetts Bay in 1630. But Grant's paternal forebears had been moving west for two centuries: from Plymouth, Massachusetts, to the Connecticut River valley, across New York State and Pennsylvania. Ulysses Grant's grandfather, Captain Noah Grant, had fought in the Revolution, lost his first wife, remarried, and moved to western Pennsylvania. Here he and Rachel built a cabin on the Monongahela River, not far from modern Pittsburgh. They raised a large family. Noah, by trade a cobbler and by character an idler, would soon move the family again: first to Fawcettstown, Ohio, on the Ohio River, thence to Deerfield in the Western Reserve.

There is a homely story—such tales cannot be authenticated— that Noah's son Jesse, the father of Ulysses Grant, just shy of his sixth birthday, came upon his mother, who was alone and weeping. "George Washington is dead," Rachel told her son. "Is he any relation of yours?" the boy asked. This was in December 1799.

Rachel died only three years later, and, in the unhappy practice of the time, the family was eventually broken up, the younger children distributed among relatives, and the eldest, Jesse included, put out to make their way on their own. Jesse was eleven.

He made his way by mother wit and determination. In adolescence Jesse's was already an avid, ambitious personality, close to the caricature of frontier Americans already familiar to English and European visitors and readers. A modern student of the Ohio of this time notes that Americans were "fidgety and nervous when not doing something that might be called work." Jesse did odd jobs, was a roustabout for three years until, by serendipity, he was hired by Judge and Mrs. George Tod to work on their farm near Youngstown. It was the making of him. He lived with the Tods for five years, growing into a young man of Gatsbyan ambition. The Tods lived comfortably and well; they read, they had nice things; they challenged, worked, educated, and inspired him. Jesse developed an unassuageable determination to become rich, to be Somebody. He read voraciously; he became a lifelong autodidact, a man of words and opinions of whom it might be said that "he never had an unuttered thought." But the boy of six who wondered whether his mother was related to George Washington would survive to see his own son twice inaugurated as president: and, at one of those inaugurals, compared to Washington himself.

Jesse moved on. He learned and worked at the tanner's trade under his half brother Peter, in Maysville, Kentucky; later with an Ohio tanner, Owen Brown, and his son (Jesse's contemporary), the future abolitionist John Brown; finally as the young partner of another Ohioan, in Ravenna, John Wells. *Tanning* to contemporary ears connotes little; it is no more helpful to our sense of its contemporary importance and standing as the fact that Saint Paul's father was a tent maker. Tanning was in fact an enormously lucrative trade in the first half of the nineteenth century. The demand for leather and worked leather goods was huge. This was a business in which, by the standards of rural Ohio, an ambitious, smart man could grow rich. The famous Galena address (*U.S. Grant, Galena, Ill.*) owes entirely to Jesse's success as a tanner whose business eventually expanded from southern Ohio to northwestern Illinois.

Jesse Grant was now twenty-three. Four years later, in June 1821, he married Hannah Simpson, the third of four children of another widower, John Simpson of Pennsylvania, who, like Captain Noah Grant, had remarried, moved west, lighting finally in Bethel, near Point Pleasant. Here he bought and worked a substantial farm, and here Jesse began his brief courtship of Hannah.

She is variously described as calm, imperturbable, taciturn, "cleanly," quietly devout in her Methodism—a natural complement to her garrulous husband. It is fair to say that in temperament and personality, in what psychiatrists call affect, Ulysses became far more his mother's than his father's son.

Hannah and Jesse would have six children, three girls and three boys, but Ulysses—the first—remained the apple of his father's eye for the first thirty years of his life, and, after a gap of several years, thereafter. He served partly as an engine of his father's ambition. Christened Hiram Ulysses (an uneasy burden at best, the "Ulysses" contracted to "Useless" during his boyhood), the son was raised in an atmosphere of easy discipline and devoted attention. Jesse always introduced or spoke of him as "my Ulysses." He doted on him. He communicated both to his son and to the town of Georgetown, the county seat to which the family moved in 1823, that he was, indeed, a child of singular gifts and destiny. The boy would succeed as Jesse was succeeding; he would be, he had to be, noticed and admired. Historians and biographers have imputed a variety of qualities of adult character to the nature of Ulysses Grant's boyhood, but their speculations often seem forced. What is known is that Jesse, a self-important bustler in a small town, bragged about Ulysses at every opportunity and was determined that he have every advantage. For her part, Hannah disbelieved in praise. She was undemonstrative in her affections; she was not a mother to whom the son could repair for understanding and compassionate counsel.

Grant's boyhood was conventional for its time, punctuated by those kinds of events and experiences that childhood friends remember much later on, when their subject has become famous. He was taught at the local subscription school; in adolescence he was sent off for one-year terms at two nearby boarding schools, the latter to prepare him for possible attendance at West Point. He was an unremarkable student: diffident and inward, watchful, reluctant to speak up. The town saw him as bashful, inferring that, because he did not talk much, he wasn't particularly bright.

He was drawn to experiences and work that challenged his practical ingenuity, such as contriving means of moving heavy rocks or logs needed for Jesse's tanning business (which the boy hated and which, no doubt, planted in him a lifetime's revulsion for the sights and smells of slaughter and blood). He evinced an early practical handiness—skill for doing, usually alone, practical things that needed to be done, taking particular pleasure in persevering until they were completed. It is not too much to argue that that quality in Grant which Lincoln most admired, and for which he was most constantly appreciative, was already visible in the boy of ten or twelve: that of not asking for help or advice, not freighting problems with imagined difficulties, but just doing them. Forty years on, when General George B. McClellan was demanding and pleading for more soldiers, Grant was asking simply, when do I start? "What I want is to advance."

His own *Memoirs* provide testimony both ironic and genial.

> One of my superstitions has always been when I started to go anywhere, or to do anything, not to have to turn back until the thing intended was accomplished. I have frequently started to go places where I had never been to and to which I did not know the way, depending upon making inquiries on the road. And if I got past the place without knowing it, instead of turning back, I would go on until a road was found turning in the right direction, take that, and come in on the other side.

Grant evinced an early love for horses that was as powerful as his revulsion from the smells and sights of the tannery. There are several recorded memories of prodigies of horsemanship and of a rare and visible ability—what today might be called horse whispering—to communicate with them. By fourteen Ulysses had established a livery service, owned and operated alone, in which the young driver would deliver passengers all over Ohio. Earlier—an incident at the very epicenter of Grant lore, adduced as an example of the boy's dullness and credulity—Ulysses had visited a Mr. Ralston to buy a horse he wanted. Jesse had authorized him to go as high as twenty-five dollars, but to try to get the animal for twenty. "Papa says I can go as high as twenty-five," the boy said to the owner, who promptly sold him the horse for twenty-five dollars. Grant historiography has generally been unkind to the child, locating flaws which will bloom grossly in later, political, life. But the anecdote may also illustrate other qualities: bottom-line directness and fairness. Grant knew the horse's worth. Nonetheless, the story achieved a wide contemporary currency, generally parsed by resentful neighbors as an example of stupidity. It is one of a small family of such tales; together they limn a portrait of a shy youngster sometimes slow on the uptake, driven in each successive encounter more and more upon his own resources, slowly becoming reluctant to say anything, to disclose to any but his closest companions his feelings and thoughts. Perhaps, as Churchill noted of his own ancestor Marlborough, such slights and twinges of adversity in youth are needed to "evoke that ruthless fixity of purpose and tenacious motherwit without which great purposes are seldom accomplished."

Several Brown County boys had already attended the United States Military Academy at West Point, and one of them, Bartlett Bailey, had attended and failed. A vacancy was thus created. Jesse applied on Ulysses's behalf, seeking the nomination from Congressman Thomas L. Hamer, a former friend whom politics had estranged—Jesse was a Whig, Hamer a Jacksonian Democrat. Hamer now obliged Jesse, in a hurried final act of the spring 1839 congressional session, sending forward the name (so he imagined it to be) "Ulysses Simpson Grant."

The son knew what was coming. Over the previous Christmas holiday Jesse had told him, "Ulysses, I believe you are going to receive your appointment."

"What appointment?"

"To West Point. I have applied for it."

"But I won't go."

In his *Memoirs*, Ulysses recalled, "He said he thought I would, and I thought so too, if he did."

Had there been an A. N. Wyeth or a Norman Rockwell in 1839, he would surely have been drawn to the scene: the youth, tiny, barely five feet tall, as apprehensive as eager, standing at the end of the dock on the shore of the gleaming broad river, entering upon an adventure that must have seemed cosmic in its dimension. No ardent patriotism or military vocation had brought Ulysses Grant to this pass. His was an opportunity unsought, an obligation laid upon him by a father with whom it would never have occurred to him to argue. The boy was game; he was curious; he seemed marked already by an easy fatalism that predisposed him to make the best of what he had been given, without complaint or undue worry. These qualities had already placed him at the observant edge of things: he was a watcher, slow in passing judgment, comfortable in going his own way, already full of the quiet self-reliance that made him act rather than explain himself. Neighbors and, much later, historians might smile at his horse whisperings, at the homely anecdotes retrofitted to make him look simple. It was widely expected that he would fail at West Point.

All his life, and in the 120 years since his death, friends, rivals and enemies, biographers, and historians have condescended to Ulysses Grant. At seventeen he already understood that he produced such an effect on smart people. Not for the last time, he struck out on his own.

2

———

A Military Education

Grant arrived at West Point on May 29, 1839. He was a young seventeen, tiny (five feet one inch, 117 pounds) and unprepossessing, too intimidated to complain that the academy authorities had perpetuated Congressman Hamer's mistake. From now on, like Harry Truman, he would have an unearned *S* for a middle initial—signifying Simpson, of course, but effacing forever, in fact and in memory, Hiram. *Ulysses Simpson Grant*: the triumphant iambic trimeter of the new name would later become a thumping proclamation of determination and victory, just as its first two initials would forever proclaim Grant's commitment to Unconditional Surrender. For the moment, older cadets, including William Tecumseh Sherman, seeing "U.S. Grant—Ohio" on the matriculation roll, made the obvious links and jibes: *U.S. Uncle Sam.* "Sam" was how Grant would be known at West Point and in the army for the next fifteen years.

In 1962 Douglas MacArthur remembered his 1894 enrollment at West Point as the fulfillment of a childhood dream. For Grant it was quite the opposite. He had not wanted to attend; he had hoped and waited, in vain, for news that the academy had been shut down.

West Point in 1839 was both young and small, having been founded only thirty-seven years earlier. It enrolled about 240 cadets, barely the size of a small boarding school. Graduating classes averaged about 45 (of the 70 or so entrants who survived their matriculation summer to begin their first year as cadets). Grant's cohort, his seven-year generation at the academy, would compose the larger part of the junior officer cadre for the army in the Mexican War (1846–48) and much of the high command, on both sides, in the Civil War. Among Grant's contemporaries at West Point were William Tecumseh Sherman (1840), James Longstreet (1842), John Pope (1842), Simon Bolivar Buckner (1842), Stonewall Jackson (1846), George B. McClellan (1846), and George Pickett (1846). In so small a school students knew one another, or knew at least the métier of virtually every other cadet—friendships in those days having been made with small regard for chronological class affiliation. That is to say, being a plebe (freshman) appears to have been less stigmatized, and much less a reason for harassment and hazing, than at later periods in the academy's history. These friendships, the general aura of intimacy, of shared hardship at an isolated army post, had powerful consequences for the graduates' estimates of one another on later active service: of what adversaries were likely to "do," in crisis or on campaign; and, equally, in the years after the Civil War, on resumed friendships and common understandings about the needs of a reunited nation. Grant as a westerner formed most of his friendships with southern boys; many of these were sustained and strengthened during the war and after.

By the late 1830s the academy had achieved a certain national cachet, although its appeal to prospective cadets and their families lay far less in its military character and mission than because attendance was free, postgraduation service requirements slight and not well enforced, and the curriculum, weighted strongly toward mathematics, the sciences, and engineering, was useful to the needs of the country in a time of robust growth and expansion. "I tell you, Coz," Cadet Grant wrote a young relative, "if a man graduates from here he is set fer life, come what may."

Cadet life was austere, regimented, unremitting in its daily demands. Living conditions were spartan. The academic curriculum, fixed and rigid, allowed no electives. Plebes studied only mathematics and French (the latter to provide facility in reading military and engineering texts); upper-class staples included topography, fortifications, engineering, physics, geography, and drawing—the last a two-year requirement, the assumption being that soldiers must be competent in drawing and sketching terrain features and preparing maps.

Cadets were given grades in all classes at all class meetings, and these grades, weighted and fed into a complicated formula that also registered disciplinary performance, determined annual and final class standing in General Order of Merit. This standing in turn determined a graduate's eligibility for appointment to the several branches of the army. The brightest, if not the best, cadets could select the Corps of Engineers; those of lower class rank went into less prestigious branches—artillery, cavalry, infantry. West Point in Grant's time, as it has been for most of its history, was obsessed with devising means to measure academic accomplishment. Its best historian, James Morrison, puts it thus: West Point "endorsed the sacrosanct . . . notion that human failure and achievement could be measured with mathematical precision."

This silly idea, long since ossified as Holy Writ, has assured that generations of famous generals, Grant among them, are celebrated for having overcome mediocre intellectual gifts in their rise to the top. In fact the connection between academic acuity as measured in such a curriculum, and fitness for high command in war, is frail indeed. The more interesting questions are these: How should aptitude for the leading of soldiers be measured in an academy whose mission is to educate cadets for such a purpose? How can the seeds of a lifelong intellectual curiosity be planted and cultivated in students who will make their careers in the profession of arms? What did Ulysses Grant do as a cadet (he was graduated twenty-first in a class of thirty-nine—mediocre, like Churchill at Harrow) when he was not laboring at his assigned courses and duties?

First, he never really labored. A roommate remembers him as a quick study, looking over his lesson once or twice before class, not especially engaged by the material—mathematics excepted. Most other subjects bored him, but the idea of returning someday to teach mathematics at West Point, in discharge of his obligation to serve, seems to have occurred to him at this time. Grant at seventeen was already a writer of confident, limber English prose. In a letter already quoted, written in the fall of 1839, he writes:

Again, if I look another way I can see Fort Putnam *frowning* far above: a stern monument to a sterner age, which seems placed there . . . to tell us of the glorious deeds of our fathers, and bid us remember their sufferings—to follow their example.

This is early evidence of the ability to write accurately and casually, a talent Grant would cultivate during an age of continuous letter writing among people separated by long distances and long periods of service. In the Civil War no commander wrote more lucid, more accurate, or more orderly communications, letters or orders, or wrote them with greater facility than Grant.

In fact his bent was toward literature. "Much of the time," he wrote in his *Memoirs*, "was devoted to novels, but not those of a trashy sort. I read all of Bulwer's then published, [James Fenimore] Cooper's, [Captain] Marryat's, [Sir Walter] Scott's, Washington Irving's works . . . and many others." Casual but voracious reading of serious fiction, well-enough remembered to be noted in a memoir by an honest writer, bore importantly on his education, as did a demonstrated facility and sensibility in sketching, watercolors, and oil.

Throughout his cadetship he was an attendant lord, never a student leader. He was promoted to the normal cadet noncommissioned ranks, corporal (as a sophomore) and sergeant (as a junior), but he said they were too much for him. Grant graduated as a cadet private. Minor disciplinary scrapes and misadventures and a manifest indifference to military rigmarole, to drum-and-trumpet militarism, shines, creases, barked commands, and posturing—such things kept him from advancing as a cadet. One of his closest undergraduate friends, James Longstreet, remembered him thus:

[His] . . . distinguished trait . . . was a girlish modesty; a taciturnity born of his own modesty; but a thoroughness in the accomplishment of whatever task was assigned him . . . his sense of honor was so perfect.

Hamlin Garland, the most important of Grant's early biographers, muses that he was cowed by the tone of West Point cadet life—the wellborn, confident southerners whose habits and sense of social superiority inflected cadet culture. Boyhood tendencies toward shyness and diffidence were accentuated and confirmed. Yet throughout his life a few very close companions were to be astonished at the Grant who unburdened himself to them, who "opened up" in private and intimate company, but who remained silent and awkward among colleagues and superiors. Contemporary views and recollections paint a more nuanced picture: "The most perfect regard for truth . . . not a prominent man in the Corps, but respected by all." "He had a way of solving problems out of rule by the application of good hard common sense."

Throughout, Cadet Grant cultivated and indulged his great continuing avocation: horses. He was known and admired as the best horseman at West Point, and later as the finest horseman in the army. He had, as we have seen, a natural affinity for horses, physical courage of the kind that is unconscious, and a wiry physique that perfectly suited the avocation. Just how extraordinary was vividly recorded by a cadet watching one of the show-and-tells that were part of nineteenth-century graduations.

It was near the end of a demonstration of riding proficiency. The academy's Master of Horse, a veteran noncommissioned officer, shouted, "Cadet Grant!"

A clean-faced, slender young fellow, weighing about one hundred twenty pounds, dashed from the ranks . . . upon a powerfully built chestnut-sorrel horse, and galloped down the opposite side of the hall. (Grant pointed the horse in the opposite direction and now) for the great leap before him, bounded into the air, carrying his rider as if man and beast were welded together. The spectators were breathless.

Just before graduation Cadet Grant learned he was to be commissioned in the infantry, with an initial assignment to Jefferson Barracks, Missouri, the army's largest post. He looked forward first to three months' leave in Ohio, then to the quiet order of garrison life and perhaps time to begin a more diligent study of mathematics, to allow a return, to teach, at West Point.

There is a Stephen Vincent Benét story, no longer much read, about a retired French officer, in failing health, who bemoans an evil fate which has denied him the only thing he has ever wanted: war. He has not commanded soldiers on active service; he has not been given the chance to test his unusual, grandiose notions of strategy. An English visitor offers the bleak comfort of a puzzled but sympathetic understanding—and, at the end of the tale, when the French officer dies, writes his epitaph. Here the reader's suspicion is confirmed: the officer is Napoleon, but a Napoleon born at the wrong time.

The class of 1843 left the academy at the right time. Little more than a year after graduation its members found themselves beginning preparations for war against Mexico: a possibility in 1844, almost a certainty by the spring of 1845. President John Tyler had asked the Senate in April 1844 to approve a motion for the annexation of Texas, and though the Senate did not oblige him, the annexation was approved the following spring by joint resolution of the Senate and the House. Mexico now broke off diplomatic relations with the United States, and, after several months' desultory and disingenuous attempts to resolve the situation favorably and peaceably, the new president, James K. Polk, contrived a casus belli: he sent an American force to the Rio Grande, claiming it (not the Nueces River, 150 miles to the north) as Texas' southern boundary. This was the beginning of what Ulysses Grant, writing forty years later in his *Memoirs*, would call "one of the most unjust [wars] ever waged by a stronger against a weaker nation . . . an instance of a republic following the bad example of European monarchies." But though perhaps doubtful of the justice of the American cause in 1844, Grant never considered resigning from the army: "Experience proves," he wrote a friend, "that the man who obstructs a war in which his nation is engaged, no matter whether right or wrong, occupies no enviable place in life or history."

Brevet (provisional) Second Lieutenant Grant reported to Jefferson Barracks, Missouri, at the end of September 1843. A long graduation furlough at home had been an idyll. Jesse had moved the family to Bethel, Ohio, a few miles from Georgetown, and here Grant recovered from a lingering illness called Tyler's Grip. He rested. He rode. And he soon did what no second lieutenant can quite resist doing: he wore his new dress uniform in public. A child in Cincinnati laughed at the getup and made mocking remarks. Grant never again risked such ridicule. Thereafter, though fastidious in matters of cleanliness, he affected indifference to army standards of dress, decoration, and protocol. The affectation, already incubating at West Point, became a settled practice, then a habit. It was a protective coloration, a way of blending in, a modest assertion of severe professional functionality. Ironically, people seeing Grant for the first time invariably would note his seedy appearance in uniform, which they sometimes took for indifference.

Jefferson Barracks was the army's largest post—home to two infantry regiments, one of them Grant's, the Fourth U.S. Infantry. The unit comprised 449 soldiers and 21 officers, most assigned to one of the regiment's eight line companies of 40 men each. The officers were regulars, the majority West Pointers; many of the soldiers were immigrants. The professional demands of garrison routine were slight and unengaging, and the post's commander, Stephen Kearney, exercised a benign, easy discipline. The officers carried out garrison duties, left most of the work to the NCOs, and were otherwise at leisure to leave post when their work was done. Most did.

Frederick Dent, Grant's roommate his last year at West Point, had not been assigned to Jefferson Barracks, but his family home, White Haven, was only five miles from the barracks. Grant and other young officers became frequent visitors at the Dents', and Grant soon began an ardent courtship of the Dents' eldest daughter, Julia, then eighteen. Her father, "Colonel" Frederick Dent, was a transplanted Marylander, southern in all his sympathies, the owner of nineteen slaves. He was irascible and bigoted. But ultimately he was no match for the auld alliance of mother and daughter, and by 1846 he had yielded with a bad grace to Grant's importunities. The couple became engaged, but with no firm date fixed for their wedding.

Julia was her father's favorite child; in the words of one of her friends, she was "as dainty a little creature as one would care to see, plump, neither tall nor short, with beautifully rounded arms, brown hair and brown eyes." She had been raised in the cosseted circumstances of her station and time, which is to say, without serious education, and was accustomed to being waited upon. She and Grant would marry soon after Grant's return from Mexico (August 1848), and theirs would prove to be an extraordinarily happy marriage.

But that was all in the future. On May 7, 1844, the Fourth Infantry was ordered to western Louisiana, near Natchitoches, as part of what was called the Army of Observation, with a primary mission to ensure that no Americans "filibustered" in Texas. Then as now, war and politics are nurseries of euphemism and obfuscation. The army's real mission, Grant remembered in the *Memoirs*, was to "serve as a menace to Mexico in case she appeared to contemplate war . . . a war that would be a conspiracy to acquire territory out of which slave states might be formed for the American Union." Grant's service in the Army of Observation gave him much pleasure; he was beginning to find elements of soldiering congenial to his temperament, as certain young men with no expectation of liking it often do. He remembered, also, his conversations with a mathematics professor at West Point, who had encouraged him to work toward a teaching assignment at the academy. Throughout these months of waiting for new orders the regiment prepared itself for what lay ahead, and, according to Grant's friend Longstreet, "since we were . . . removed from all society without books or papers . . . we had an excellent opportunity of studying each other." Grant studied no one so carefully as his new commanding officer, Brevet Brigadier General Zachary Taylor, whose methods of command and whose presentation of himself as a leader confirmed Grant's own ideas of leadership; they lodged in his memory an indelible model of leadership to be emulated. Taylor was a big, rumpled figure, like Grant indifferent to claims of spruceness and military rigmarole. He wore what he pleased, liked to talk about subjects other than war and armies, and would sit his horse sidesaddle, in blue jeans and a linen duster, observing training or directing battle.

Taylor's force was ordered to Texas in June 1845. The Army of

Occupation, as it was now called, augmented to some four thousand regulars, deployed in five infantry regiments, was to move to Corpus Christi, at the mouth of the Nueces River, then march overland, south to the Rio Grande. President Polk was determined that Mexico, not the United States, provide the occasion for war. The Mexicans soon obliged him, killing several Americans on a reconnaissance mission near the river. The war's opening engagement, at Palo Alto on May 8, 1846, seems less a battle than a staged encounter between two small armies anxious to probe, then test, the other's strength. Taylor's force, perhaps two thousand men, confronted a Mexican army twice its size. The whole action wore the air of an eighteenth-century European encounter, the Mexicans quietly observing the linear deployment of Taylor's force, refraining from attacking, while the Americans were making ready, aligning their ranks (companies on line, with artillery batteries between them), sending men to the rear to fill canteens. The field of battle itself was a wide and treeless plain, much of it deep in grass.

Mexican artillery opened the battle, firing solid shot, the course of the balls eerily visible to the Americans—in the air and as they cut paths through the grasses around them—which must have lent a surreal, slow-motion aura to Lieutenant Grant's first experience of combat. It was at once plain that the enemy's guns lacked sufficient range to inflict serious damage, and that its gun crews were not terribly efficient. The signal was given for Taylor's artillery to respond, and it did so, firing larger-caliber shells, all explosive shells, many of them finding their targets with telling accuracy. General Taylor soon gave the order for his right-flank companies, Grant's included, to charge the Mexican infantry. They did so; the enemy force retreated before them, withdrawing early that night.

Lieutenant Grant had now come under fire; he had seen (and soon described in letters home) his first American casualty, Captain John Page. But like any young soldier, Grant was as much interested in how he would behave under fire, how he would react to it, as he was determined to master whatever fears the battle would excite. He found that he had far less fear than he imagined he would have—and wrote a friend in Ohio: "You want to know what my feelings were on the field of battle. I do not know that I felt any particular sensation. War seems much less horrible to persons engaged in it than to those who read of the battles." Grant also noted, not without admiration, the stolidity and discipline of his enemy's common soldiers; and the inefficiency of the Mexican officers, their lack of fellow feeling for the men they commanded, their remoteness from them. All his life Grant would be a student of the relations between those in authority and those whom circumstance obliged to obey.

The fighting resumed the next day at Resaca de la Palma, nearer the Rio Grande. For a while Grant was in temporary command of an infantry company, which, having made a successful charge, believed it had captured several Mexican soldiers, including a colonel. Later it was discovered that the men they captured were already prisoners. The Mexican army retreated across the river, again having sustained very heavy casualties.

Over the next three months thousands of volunteers began to arrive from the United States, eager to join Taylor's army and see something of the fighting. Taylor chose not to advance until they had been trained and their units assigned specific duties for the campaign, now against a much larger enemy force defending the important fortress city of Monterrey, some 125 miles away. Grant was relieved peremptorily of his duties as a line officer and assigned as quartermaster for the Fourth Infantry, a position of large responsibility for a lieutenant barely twenty-four. He protested vigorously: "I respectfully protest against being assigned to a duty which removes me from sharing in the dangers and honors of service with my company at the front, and respectfully ask to be permitted to resume my place in line."

The regimental commander, Brevet Colonel John Garland, responded stiffly in the negative, softening his message by noting that Lieutenant Grant had shown "ability, skill, and persistency in the line of duty."

Whether the appointment was serendipitous, or whether Garland really knew his man, Grant proved to be an extraordinary logistician. Necessity, Jacob Bronowski wrote, is the mother not of invention but of improvisation, and nothing could more mercilessly and continuously try Grant's skills at improvisation than the demands of feeding, moving, and supplying an infantry regiment on campaign in a difficult enemy country. It was exactly the kind of experience as a young officer that Wellington gained in India, thirty years before he fought the French; it would prove as useful to Grant as it did to Wellington. He could now demonstrate the skills he had begun to hone in adolescence in Ohio. He was resourceful and independent; his temperament was of the kind to which exasperation is foreign. And conceivably Colonel Garland understood that an aggressive young quartermaster officer could easily contrive to escape his staff responsibilities when the regiment was engaged in battle.

The historian Brooks Simpson has called Monterrey (September 21–23, 1846) the first serious battle of the Mexican War. Grant joined Garland's brigade in a charge against the well-defended eastern walls of the city—a charge that resulted in one-third of the Fourth Infantry Regiment becoming casualties, including the regimental adjutant, Grant's friend Charles Hoskins. Grant temporarily succeeded Hoskins, as the brigade disengaged, acting as adjutant until a successor could be appointed. Another charge by the Americans was equally costly—the Mexicans firing canister from fortified positions: "It was as if bushels of hickory nuts were hurled at us."

Contemporaries provide two other glimpses of Grant. One, of Grant tenderly ministering to wounded Americans left on the battlefield that night; the second, of Grant's volunteer mission to ride to the divisional supply depot to secure more ammunition for the brigade. Here his supreme skill as a rider probably saved his life and made possible the relief of the unit: Grant braved direct fire from the streets of Monterrey, riding like a movie cowboy, hanging by stirrups and cantle, keeping the horse's massive body between himself and the enemy. It was an exploit remembered vividly by all who watched it.

Taylor offered terms to the Mexican defenders of the city, allowing the defeated force under General Ampudia to march out under their flags. But the surrender did not cause the Mexican government to seek a general settlement. Taylor's army remained around the city for several months, training the volunteer regiments now joining.

Grant continued as regimental quartermaster, mourned the deaths of young officer friends, and wrote ardent, earnest letters to Julia. He formed a brief friendship with Thomas L. Hamer, the Ohio congressman who had appointed him to West Point seven years earlier. Hamer had come to Mexico with the brevet rank of brigadier general of volunteers, had looked up Grant, and saw enough of him to make the not quite objective pronouncement that his appointee had become "a most remarkable and valuable young soldier." Hamer "anticipate[d] for him a brilliant future, if he should have the opportunity to display his powers when they mature."

Anxious lest Taylor's star shine too brightly, President Polk now appointed General Winfield Scott as American commander in Mexico, endorsing Scott's plan to capture the Gulf port of Vera Cruz and then march some 240 miles, to Mexico City, the capital. As a strategic objective Mexico City stands direct comparison with Richmond in 1864: in each case the enemy army, not the capital, was the real objective, the assumption being that the enemy armies would interpose between the U.S. Army and the capital cities, and a battle with definitive results would follow. The capitals would, simply, fall.

Scott's force, ten thousand soldiers on a huge polyglot flotilla, appeared off Vera Cruz in March 1847. The army landed unopposed and settled down to a siege and bombardment of the city. The garrison commander obliged the Americans by surrendering, and on March 29 the defeated Mexicans marched away, honor intact, flags uncased, the officers allowed to retain their personal weapons and horses. Like Taylor at Monterrey, Scott at Vera Cruz understood the uses of magnanimity, but with the cynical expectation that the paroled officers would urge their countrymen to insist on a negotiated peace with the United States.

Wellington is reported to have said that the Scott expedition's march to Mexico City and its capture of the city was a feat unparalleled in modern war. The army marched across difficult terrain, fought a successful battle high in the mountains at Cerro Gordon, then, completely removed from its base of supply, struck out for the capital, living off the land (which put a premium on the quartermaster's ability and diligence), all the while fighting off guerrillas. After an initial exchange with the enemy, just outside the city, Scott ordered a truce, again in the hope that the Mexicans would ask for terms. They did not; rather, the enemy commander Santa Anna reinforced his positions at the fortress of Chapultepec and at Molina del Rey and, at the northwest limit of the city, San Cosme. The American force could not advance into the city while Mexican troops dominated this position. An initial American assault, in which Grant participated, was stopped cold. Now Grant and several other soldiers, noticing a church steeple within firing distance of the Mexican position, disassembled a howitzer, insisted a priest allow them entry into the church, mounted the reassembled weapon in the church belfry, and opened fire on the Mexican position below. By the next day, American arms were everywhere successful, Mexican resistance throughout the city had crumbled, and the government asked for terms.

Mexico was radically shrunk by the Treaty of Guadalupe Hidalgo, which formally ended the war. It recognized American sovereignty at the north bank of the Rio Grande and ceded to the United States almost all of modern-day New Mexico, Arizona, and California. In return the United States gave up its claim to Baja California, agreed to assume all claims against Mexico by American citizens, and to pay Mexico fifteen million dollars. The army's victory did not mean immediate homecoming and demobilization. Grant and the Fourth Infantry did not return to Jefferson Barracks until the summer of 1848. In the intervening months, a time of easy garrison duty, he explored Mexico, studied its language and its people. Grant took from the war an abiding love for Mexico, its people and its land; an accumulating unease with the decisions that had led to the war; and qualms about the war itself, the bloodiest in American history up to that point.

Mexico was also a proving ground, an extended live-fire exercise for a generation of company-grade officers, mostly in their twenties, who would furnish the division, corps, and army commanders of both Confederate and Union forces in the Civil War. During the war and in its aftermath, Grant came to know many of them well— officers who, in fifteen years, would be comrades and enemies in the

Civil War. The majority of Grant's friends in Mexico were south-erners (they made up about two-thirds of the American regulars and volunteers), and if not southerners, with rare exceptions, coun-try boys from the West, the kinds of young men with whom Grant was comfortable. Some, later on, would have dramatic encounters with Grant: Simon Bolivar Buckner, who would surrender Fort Donelson to him in 1862; John C. Pemberton, who would surren-der Vicksburg in 1863; James Longstreet, who would be best man in Grant's wedding in 1848, and, at Appomattox, the first old friend to greet him as he walked toward the McClean House to accept Lee's surrender.

"We studied each other," as Longstreet had noted of service in Louisiana before the war. Grant studied Taylor, certainly, and Scott, contrasting their leadership styles, admiring both but favoring Tay-lor. Consciously and unconsciously he also studied himself, and it is plain that Grant's trust in his own ability as a soldier was con-firmed. He was hugely but modestly self-reliant; he was accus-tomed to making do with what he was given, without asking for more; he defined himself in action, not talk; he was dutiful, intensely loyal to superiors and friends, brave in the way that Taci-tus called Agricola brave: unconsciously so. All these qualities would go, in the fullness of time, to the making of a great fighting general. Whether they would together be suitable to a successful president could not begin to be known until four years after the Civil War had ended.

3

Peace Is Hell

In no profession do the attractions and rewards of action differ so profoundly from those of training and preparation as they do in soldiering. The differences between active service in war and in peace are as obvious as they are fundamental.

Grant had been exhilarated by the demands of his service in the Mexican War, but his next assignments promised little of the excitement of combat. Following his marriage to Julia Dent on August 22, 1848, Grant had expected to resume his old job as a regimental quartermaster, this time in Detroit, but he arrived to find another staff officer assigned those duties, and a new commanding officer, a superannuated colonel who had missed service in Mexico altogether. Grant was ordered to Madison Barracks in Sackets Harbor, New York, on the shore of Lake Ontario, and here he and Julia spent the next five—winter—months, returning to Detroit in the spring of 1849.

As a peacetime quartermaster Lieutenant Grant was essentially nothing more than a commissioned clerk, bored and unchallenged in a position for which he was ill suited. He wrote later: "I was no clerk, nor had I any capacity to become one." When a young soldier complained about Grant's office inefficiencies, a sergeant who had known Grant in Mexico rejoined that here was a real soldier, a natural leader of troops in battle; he should not be judged by the expectations of garrison bureaucrats. Like other officers of his time, Grant filled up his hours by indulging other interests and avocations. He kept, and raced, horses; he explored the lands along the border with Canada; he visited West Point.

A few army colleagues described him as a young man at the edge of things (just as he had been at West Point): quiet, watchful, following his own drum; merely competent at work; unusually devoted to his wife, who gave birth to their first child, Frederick, in May 1850. Unstirred by certain kinds of challenges, things that might somehow have engaged him fully, he had become again the passive young man all but his closest friends remembered: alone in a crowd, unremarkable, and silent. It was known that he had joined a local Sons of Temperance Lodge (in Sackets Harbor)—an affiliation indicating, probably, that Grant had had a session or two with an older friend (a minister perhaps), who had gently admonished him to watch his drinking. But no one would have known this better than Grant himself; and it had yet to become an issue.

A contemporary of Grant's in Detroit, an army officer named James Pitman, has left a vivid description of the young officer of 1849. "He always had an abstract air about him . . . he was like a trained athlete, who leans listless and indifferent against the wall, but who wakes to wonders when the call is made upon him . . . he was a young man who seemed older than he was by reason of his gravity and reticence."

In early 1852, with little warning, the Fourth Infantry Regiment was ordered to California, whose population had tripled since the beginning of the Gold Rush in 1849. A military presence was required, and as quartermaster Grant was responsible for the movement of the regiment. Julia had tried to persuade Ulysses that she and the baby should accompany him—and she was again pregnant—but each must have known how foolhardy such a passage would have been. Instead, she returned to White Haven to wait on events; the nineteenth-century army had neither a rotation policy nor a standard deployment length. A rueful "I'll see you when I see you" was the only honest farewell a soldier and his family could exchange.

The eight-day journey to Panama was merely uncomfortable. Now, landing at Colón, on the Gulf coast, the regiment undertook a trip from hell, a journey across the isthmus which was then in the midst of a cholera epidemic. Of preventive counsel, contemporary medicine could offer nothing more useful than "Don't drink the water"; treatment consisted of cold compresses and praying, neither promising reliable results. Of the 700 members of the Fourth Infantry party, only 450 made it safely across; seventeen of the twenty small children among the dependents died en route.

Grant had been assigned to command the second of the two regimental parties—the dependents and baggage. The climate was humid, the heat searing, the rains unending. Transportation requisitioned did not materialize. Half the traverse was made in dugout canoes poled by naked natives; the rest, across dangerous passes, on mules that Grant hired en route. Survivors credited him with heroic, tireless labor and unfailing resourcefulness: "He was like a ministering angel to all," said one.

Fort Vancouver, in the Oregon Territory several miles down the Columbia River from Portland, had been selected as regimental headquarters, and the companies were assigned smaller posts about the Pacific Northwest. Grant continued his duties as regimental quartermaster: the procurement and distribution of supplies, the maintenance of accounts and property, an occasional fitting-out of surveying expeditions from the East.

The site was beautiful and bracing. But Grant's experience at Vancouver and at the smaller post to which he was assigned soon afterward, Fort Humboldt, soon became bleak. Without Julia and Fred he was miserable. His work did not engage him, and he had little interest in hunting or fishing. Moreover, he was without funds, and he failed at every extracurricular business venture in which he enlisted—going into partnership in a general store, cutting ice and sending it south by ship for sale in San Francisco, planting a large acreage in potatoes, leasing space for a men's club in San Francisco. He had tried them with the idea of raising money enough to bring Julia and Fred and his new baby son, Ulysses, Jr., out to the Pacific coast. But given his experience on the isthmus, he decided the venture was improvident if not impossible. Lonely and discouraged, he began to drink regularly, and often alone. As a small man his capacity was perilously limited; a single glass of whiskey slurred his speech; more, and he became obviously drunk.

It is during these days that Grant's reputation as a man with an alcohol problem was established, and in the tiny peacetime army, in which all officers knew or knew about all others, word of his drinking spread easily. Certain circumstances proved especially damaging: George McClellan, then an engineer lieutenant, came to Fort Vancouver in late June 1853, and it was Grant's duty to supervise the preparations necessary to his explorations in the mountains thereabouts. A friend remembered that Grant "got on one of his little sprees, which annoyed and offended" the priggish careerist McClellan, who "never quite forgave Grant for it."

Though Grant was promoted to captain in August 1853, he was becoming progressively more depressed and despairing on the West Coast. By this time he had been transferred to Fort Humboldt, some 250 miles north of San Francisco, on a bleak, remote promontory overlooking a bay of the Pacific. Here those elements that together had already brought him to the verge of despair were multiplied. Indeed it is difficult to imagine a setting and an assignment less congenial, ultimately more debilitating, to a young man of Ulysses Grant's temperament, preoccupations, and (by now) well-established habit of seeking refuge from loneliness in liquor. He was without engaging companionship, desperately lonely for Julia and his boys (one of whom he had never seen), without reliable assurance as to when he might be reassigned, a servitor in peacetime army duty that promised nothing. Circumstances had contrived an impossible situation for him. Worse, his new commanding officer was Brevet Lieutenant Colonel Robert C. Buchanan, a martinet with whom Grant had once had an unpleasant encounter at Jefferson Barracks over an idle matter of mess decorum. The circumstances at Fort Humboldt remain obscure, but it appears that Buchanan, hearing stories about Grant's drinking, warned him that a further offense would bring severe discipline, perhaps even leading to dismissal from the army.

The offense came that spring. Grant was reported the worse for wear at the pay table, where he was on duty disbursing the men's monthly pay. Buchanan called him in and gave him the option of resigning from the army.

Grant did so at once, on April 11, 1854.

On his way home (to White Haven) he found himself broke in New York City and asked Captain Simon Bolivar Buckner, then serving in the city, to arrange a loan to pay his hotel bill and see him back to Missouri. Buckner obliged (Grant repaying him in funds furnished from Jesse)—an act of kindness to be remembered eight years later. Meantime Jesse had written the secretary of war, Jefferson Davis, asking that his son's resignation be understood as a request for a furlough—that it had been the act of a man too long away from his family, and who, in reconsideration, would surely have thought better of what he had done. But Davis was unmoved. Jesse's outrage lay in his consideration of how his son's resignation from the army, after his constant bragging on him, would make him—Jesse—look.

Grant arrived home in August 1854, to Julia and the little boys he did not know. From that date until the spring of 1861 (a period historians conventionally treat as a tedious longueur of "failure" in Grant's life), the family lived at White Haven and, after May 1860, in Galena, Illinois. Jesse had offered his son a job there in 1854, after his resignation, working in the leather goods store he had established some years earlier, and which employed Ulysses's two younger brothers, but Ulysses turned him down. The father had then attached a strange, peremptory demand: that Julia and the little boys remain with *him*, in Covington, Kentucky.

Rather, they moved into a house on the Dent property in Missouri. Ulysses began farming the sixty acres that Colonel Dent had given Julia as a wedding present. Grant threw himself into the work with delight. Its yield, particularly in a time of agricultural depression, was far from sufficient to sustain the family, and Grant supplemented it by cutting firewood, hauling it into St. Louis, and selling it on the street. He was a young man (still in his early thirties), to whom his young family was everything, a man willing to try various trades and professions until one proved satisfying and remunerative. He had always liked the idea of farming; by temperament he was happiest working alone or with a few trusted friends. In this spirit he undertook to build a house, on the same land; eighteen months' enterprise completed it in 1856. He called it "Hardscrabble." Meantime he also worked on Colonel Dent's land, supervising the colonel's slaves. In 1859 he bought one of them from Dent and gave the man his freedom months later. As a supervisor he was unsatisfactory, by the common standards of the day, in that he was too softhearted and kind—too generous in his payments of men who did work for him.

Sightings and glimpses of him were reported by old friends from Jefferson Barracks or by officers passing through St. Louis, Grant invariably described as down on his luck. The year 1857 was perhaps the low point: it was a time of severe agricultural depression, and Grant pawned his gold watch to buy Christmas presents for the family. Soon after, he joined one of the Dent cousins, Harry Boggs, in St. Louis, in the latter's real estate and rent collection business— another dead end, work for which Grant seemed superlatively ill qualified. He served briefly in a customhouse—having failed in his application for the position of county engineer, probably on the grounds that, as Colonel Dent's son-in-law, he must be a Democrat, and such positions are almost always made with party affiliations in mind. (Grant had in fact voted in 1856—the only election in which he is known to have voted: he cast his ballot for the Democratic candidate, James Buchanan. About the Republican nominee, John C. Frémont, Grant would say only, "I knew Frémont.")

The family continued to grow. Two other children were born— Nellie in 1855 and Jesse in 1858—and it was at this time, almost providentially, that Grant's father renewed his offer of a job at the leather store in Galena, even knowing that, as he said, "The Army had ruined him for business." But Simpson, the elder of the two brothers at the store, was in failing health; Orvil, more ambitious and active, was only twenty-four. There was work to be done. Ulysses Grant and his family arrived in Galena in May 1860.

4

"I Propose to Move Upon Your Works"

The Civil War was the most terrible in our history. In the century between Waterloo (1815) and the beginning of World War I (1914) its costs, measured in blood and suffering, were the greatest of any of the world's wars. Deaths attributable to combat, both sides together, were 698,000; adding in the wounded, the casualty total is 1,168,000, or 1.9 percent of the population of the United States. The equivalent percentage today, given the current American population, would be just over 5,400,000 casualties. Ignorant armies of boys and young men, led mainly by volunteer officers appointed for reasons that had nothing to do with their fitness to lead soldiers in battle, tore at one another, employing the baffled, suicidal tactics of the day.

We no longer really grasp this. The numbers both overwhelm and numb our capacity to respond. Thousands died in single battles, often soldiers from the same towns or counties—their regiments having been recruited by appeals to local pride and patriotism. At Shiloh, April 6–7, 1862, total casualties were greater than all losses in all American wars up to that date: twenty-three thousand killed, wounded, or missing. Grant wrote:

> I saw an open field . . . over which the Confederates had made repeated charges . . . so covered with dead that it

would have been possible to walk across the clearing in any direction, stepping on dead bodies, without a foot touching the ground.

This statement in its particulars was not uncommon.

Long since, a softening haze of romance has descended over all this horror, obscuring our view and enfeebling our capacity to see the war whole. Films deliver sanitized depictions of linear charges and soldiers who "fall." Novelists and historians employ the ancient machinery of synecdoche: Lee attacked at 3 p.m. Sheridan charged at dusk. A cloud of dust indicated Longstreet was en route. The commander's name is used as shorthand for fifteen thousand men, a quarter to be killed by the end of the action.

The most capable general of the war achieved his successes precisely because he could—as we would say today—deal with such chaos, could respond to the slaughter, the hideous costs, in ways that approached a certain kind of calm objectivity; that is to say, by an intelligent, fast (but unhurried) consideration of all factors that bore on whatever situation was presented to him: aims, resources, terrain, distances, enemy capabilities, the locations and abilities of subordinate commanders, the fitness and morale of the troops—his own and his enemy's. Grant was willing to make decisions and live with their consequences, sustained, as William Tecumseh Sherman once said, by a constant faith in victory. Such an ability grew from the same source as its concomitants: the predisposition to do the thing required with the resources available, and to do it as quickly as possible; to act, not to talk, to give oneself uncalculatedly to the work.

Within eight months of his reentering the army, Grant became a national hero as a consequence of his brilliant victory at Fort Donelson. Thereafter, during the remaining three years of war, he was seen, always and everywhere, as the Union general most apt to attack the enemy, to persist in the attack, and with the best chance of success. Like the hero of Tennyson's "Ulysses," Ulysses Grant was always impatient to engage: "How dull it is to pause, to rust unburnished, not to shine in use!" This is close kin to "What I want is to advance." He was not a commanding presence but a functional soldier whose absorption in his work was so complete that it scoured away considerations of personal advantage, risk, or danger. These things, and an unfailing autonomy, were what would commend him to Abraham Lincoln and what would sustain Lincoln's unwavering loyalty to Grant.

It is wrong to attribute Grant's success to a sudden transformation of character or to the serendipity of finding himself in a profession, and time, in which his abilities would suddenly and startlingly reveal themselves. Grant did not change; he learned and grew; the units he commanded, in achieving small tactical successes early in the war, began to believe in him and in themselves. Far better than other Union commanders, Grant understood how to get men to do what he wanted them to do, and this quality led him to the victories that propelled him to his early fame. There was an elemental ordinariness to him that his soldiers liked and that made their relationship easy and productive. A century later he might have been a reserve colonel, crouching on Omaha Beach alongside the sons of men whose fathers were friends from the office. Grant's character fitted him perfectly to the needs of his profession and his place in it—wartime military leadership among midwestern townsmen and farmers. And another cliché fits well: he did find himself in the right place at the right time.

"Galena" is a label that lives vaguely in the public consciousness of Ulysses Grant's life, like his drinking or his heavy wartime casualties, or "Appomattox": that is, from a clerkship in Galena he went on to military glory as triumphant leader of Union armies in the Civil War.

In May 1860, the Grants arrived in the small river town, where Ulysses worked in the leather goods store established by his father but now managed by his younger brothers Simpson and Orvil. His duties were negligible, his hours regular, his trips away (to see wholesalers) infrequent. The job's prospects were not exciting, but the work permitted him a life of domestic felicity such as he and Julia had never enjoyed before, and such a life Grant gratefully embraced, as he embraced his family each night. It would not last long.

Following the election of Abraham Lincoln, South Carolina seceded from the Union on December 20, 1860, to be followed by six more southern states over the next two months. On April 15, 1861, Galena learned of the surrender of Fort Sumter, in Charleston Harbor; the next day Lincoln called for seventy-five thousand volunteers to put down the rebellion. At a town meeting former captain Grant was asked by citizens to preside while the community debated what its response should be, a meeting in which a young lawyer, John Rawlins, made a passionate speech—there are now only "traitors and patriots," which will you be?—and in which the local congressman, a transplanted New Englander named Elihu Washburne, probably looked hard at Ulysses Grant for the first time.

Like hundreds of northern towns, Galena at once committed itself to raising a volunteer company. Grant, though neither prominent nor ambitious, suddenly became the local authority on what to do. It was remembered that he was a West Point graduate and a Mexican War veteran. He drilled the men but declined to be their commander, merely following along, in civilian clothes, when the company was marched off to the state capital at Springfield. Here they joined tens of thousands of other volunteers. Grant wrote his father (then living in Covington, Kentucky):

> We are now in the midst of trying times when every one must be for or against his country, and show his colors by his every act. . . . I do not wish to act hastily or inadvisably in the matter, and as there are more than enough to respond to the first call of the President, I have not yet offered myself.

Over the next eight weeks he made himself useful as an assistant in the governor's office and as a mustering-in officer, but he remained a civilian. Grant's services were quiet, efficient, and obliging—and menial. To the few who noticed him, Grant seemed oddly unambitious, a man without the restless vanity that craves recognition and lobbies for promotion. In his travels around the state he did make certain quiet efforts to remind superiors of his skills: He prepared and mailed a letter to the adjutant general in Washington; the letter was never answered. He spent two days in a waiting room, hoping to be interviewed by Major General George McClellan—who, though he knew Grant was there, declined to see him. Yet Grant refused a West Point contemporary's offer to help him secure a commission—"I declined to receive endorsement for permission to fight for my country."

"The office must seek the man," the saying goes. Whether this was a sentiment consciously embraced or the protective coloration of a young man already bruised too many times, the question became moot on June 16, 1861, when Richard Yates, the governor of Illinois, appointed Grant colonel of the Twenty-first Regiment of Illinois volunteers, on the advice of a colleague who told him the way to get Grant to do something was simply to tell him to do it.

The narrative of Grant's rise, from colonel of volunteers to Union hero (eight months later) and to general in chief (two years after that), has been rehearsed hundreds of times, usually as an inversion of the familiar Peter Principle. Grant was raised up quickly in successive promotions simply because the nature of his aptitudes and skills demanded such promotions: he succeeded repeatedly in battle, and at a time when all other Union generals were failing—and always making excuses for their failures. To citizens in the East who knew almost nothing of Grant except that he was winning, his feats were gratefully celebrated; his reputation as a fighting general soon spread all over the country.

In the summer of 1861, however, Grant was training and leading the Twenty-first Illinois in operations against guerrilla forces in Missouri. Here was an ideal tactical crucible. When Grant was first introduced to his regiment (a notoriously fractious collection of youngbloods and skylarkers who had volunteered for ninety days' service), he had no uniform and no horse. At the end of two emotional harangues by Illinois congressmen who had also taken volunteer commissions, he merely stepped forward and said, "Men, go to your quarters." The next day he began giving quiet, simple directions, insisting they be executed efficiently and promptly, *prompt* being a favored word in the Grant vocabulary. Curfews and standards of appearance, conduct, and military deportment were enforced. There was no posturing or shouting, simply a communicated, anodyne competence. Here was a man perfectly fitted to the needs of his profession, commanding volunteer soldiers in a democratic republic in time of war.

Operations in Missouri provided the regiment and its commander a taste of combat, and it instructed both commander and commanded in many other ways useful to their service later on. Grant began to assemble a staff. He looked for quiet, easy competence lightly worn—except in his chief of staff, the fierce, demanding (and protective) John Rawlins. Later he recorded his own most important lesson. The Twenty-first, ordered by Grant's commander, John C. Frémont, to engage a Confederate force under Colonel Thomas Harris, made a long forced march to the putative location of the enemy near the village of Florida, Missouri. Then:

> As we approached the brow of the hill from which it was expected we would see Harris' camp, and possibly find his men ready formed to meet us, my heart kept getting higher and higher until it felt to me as though it was in my throat. I would have given anything then to have been back in Illinois, but I had not the moral courage to halt and consider what to do; I kept right on. When we reached a point from which the valley below was in full view I halted. The place where Harris had been encamped a few days before was still there and the marks of a recent encampment were plainly visible, but the troops had gone. My heart resumed its place. It occurred to me at once that Harris had been as much afraid of me as I had been of him. This was a view of the question I had never taken before; but it was one I never forgot afterwards. From that event to the close of the war, I never experienced trepidation upon confronting an enemy.

A few days later the regimental chaplain told him that he had read in a St. Louis paper that Grant had been promoted to brigadier general. Congress had authorized sixteen new brigadiers; Illinois had been granted four, and the senior member of the House of Representatives, the Galena congressman Elihu Washburne, had sent Grant's name forward. He was ranked first of the four. Washburne had already identified Grant as a comer; the promotion gave the new general the singular satisfaction of its having come unsought, and it represented another step in the relationship that would soon prove useful to both men.

On August 27 Frémont ordered Grant to assume command of all Union troops in southern Illinois and southeastern Missouri, with headquarters at Cairo, Illinois, at the junction of the Mississippi and Ohio rivers. The historian Jean Edward Smith calls the appointment "a benchmark in American history, akin to FDR's selection of Eisenhower to lead the Normandy invasion." Frémont (soon to be relieved by President Lincoln for his precipitate and unauthorized emancipation of all slaves in Kentucky) had a keen strategic sense of what would win the war in the West: control of the Mississippi system—the main river itself and the wide navigable tributaries that emptied into it, the Ohio most importantly; and the Cumberland and Tennessee rivers that flowed north into the Ohio, their junctions at Smithland and Paducah, Kentucky. To control the Mississippi from New Orleans to Cairo was to isolate the Confederacy from the trans-Mississippi West, and to deny its use to the South; to control the Cumberland and the Tennessee was to dominate the two major axes of advance into the Deep South, into Tennessee, Alabama, and Mississippi.

Frémont wanted Grant to capture the Mississippi River fortress town of Columbus, Kentucky, a railway terminus that linked the area to the Gulf coast, but—here is serendipity—the Confederate general Leonidas Polk acted too soon. Polk's capture of Columbus, violating the state's neutrality, prompted the state legislature to resolve to expel the rebel invaders. Grant responded instantly, embarking a force of infantry and artillery onto river steamers, sailing the flotilla

to Paducah, forty-five miles upriver on the Ohio, at its juncture
with the Tennessee. The force took over the city—which had
expected momentarily to be occupied by Polk's army marching
over from Columbus. Grant issued a proclamation, a declaration
both ardent and unbureaucratic in tone and language:

> Citizens of Paducah! I have come among you, not as an
> enemy, but as your friend and fellow-citizen, not to injure or
> annoy you, but to respect the rights . . . of all loyal citi-
> zens. . . . I am here to defend you against [this] enemy. . . . *I
> have nothing to do with opinions.* I shall deal only with armed
> rebellion and its aiders and abettors.

Grant had not sought Frémont's permission to capture Paducah,
though Frémont had already sent word that he would support such
a move should it be proposed. Less than three months later, on
November 5, Grant and a riverine force of several ships and three
thousand soldiers got under way; their objective now was the Missouri town of Belmont, just across the river from Columbus, Kentucky. Frémont had asked Grant to "demonstrate," but Grant
resolved to attack and capture the Confederate garrison encamped
there. Grant was not well suited to demonstrations.

Five Union regiments and supporting artillery landed about
three miles north of Belmont, on the west side of the Mississippi,
around 8:30 a.m. on November 6. After a rapid forced march to
Belmont, the regiments deployed in line abreast, artillery dispersed
among them, a small cavalry force on the flank. An artillery barrage
scattered the Confederate force, which fled toward the river. A cel-
ebration ensued: a band played, the troops ransacked the rebel
camp, carrying off souvenirs—just as, quietly unnoticed, five more
Confederate regiments landed between Grant's point of disem-
barkation and Belmont itself. The Union force was obliged to fight
its way out of its celebratory chaos.

The North called Belmont a victory; in a sense it was. A Union
force under a young general had fought with a ferocity and courage
that reassured people that its soldiers could succeed if capably led.

But as Grant's best biographer has pointed out, it revealed a certain tactical deficiency in Grant's temperament: in his determination to attack, he tended to ignore enemy capabilities and resources; he did not pause to consider what his enemy was likely to do—unless it was to make the facile assumption that they would not attack.

Belmont was inconclusive, its tactical significance meager. Losses were about the same on both sides. But the battle provided Grant confidence in himself as commander, and fresh confidence in the volunteer soldiers he had trained and led. He would learn the obvious lesson: no battle is won until the enemy force or its will has been destroyed utterly. For their part, the troops of this small ad hoc force now saw that they could fight rebel soldiers and beat them.

They had seen their general in action and had faith in him: he was without apparent fear; he was coolly efficient, imperturbable—and resourceful. He knew what to do, and much of what he had done he did where they could see it. Grant was the last man to leave the Belmont battlefield, his horse clambering down a narrow gangplank onto the last steamer pulling away from the shore.

Columbus, Kentucky, represented the western anchor of the trans-Allegheny Confederate line—which ran, roughly, east through Bowling Green, thence all the way to the Cumberland Gap. About halfway between Columbus and Bowling Green the two major tributaries of the Ohio (the Tennessee and the Cumberland) run north, parallel with each other and, for a stretch, barely twelve miles apart. These rivers offered obvious invasion routes into the Deep South—into Alabama and northern Mississippi, and also, via the Cumberland, directly into Nashville. The Confederates had established forts commanding the two rivers, Fort Henry on the eastern shore of the Tennessee and Fort Donelson on the western shore of the Cumberland, each guarding against prospective naval or amphibious forays upriver.

Grant and his naval colleague Flag Officer Andrew Foote had made a reconnaissance a month earlier: they had seen Fort Henry and were convinced it could be taken easily. In January 1862 Grant visited St. Louis to see his superior, Major General Henry W. "Old Brains" Halleck, who had succeeded Frémont, and to make the case for an immediate attack on Fort Henry. Halleck turned him down peremptorily, and with such brio that Grant returned to Cairo wondering what he had said or done. In fact he had done nothing wrong. Halleck simply had the staff officer's suspicion of an aggressive field commander; he wanted to control and direct things himself. A few weeks later, Foote now joining Grant in urging the case for an attack, Halleck acceded—possibly because of Halleck's perception that a rival, Major General Don Carlos Buell, was making good progress in eastern Kentucky, and because of reports that strong reinforcements under Confederate general P. G. T. Beauregard were en route to Mississippi and the western theater.

Halleck was also now aware of President Lincoln's General Order #1, which ordered an advance on all Union fronts immediately—and among those fronts mentioned was that of the "Army and Flotilla at Cairo." Grant's force exceeded fifteen thousand men, split between two ad hoc divisions: one under John McClernand, and the other under Brigadier General Charles F. Smith, Grant's former West Point commandant.

Fort Henry fell almost immediately. The historian Spencer Tucker quotes a Confederate captain: "We had a more dangerous force to contend with than the Federals—namely the river itself." Not only did the fort lack its full complement of men and artillery; its site actually placed it *lower* than enemy ships riding at high water. Late on the morning of February 6, 1862, Grant's division landed near the fort, with Smith's division occupying the high ground across the river, and Foote's flat-bottomed gunboats opened up. By midafternoon the Confederate commander had no choice but to surrender; most of his garrison of more than three thousand escaped east, to Fort Donelson, twelve miles away. The river was now open, all the way to Muscle Shoals, Alabama.

On the twelfth Grant marched his force across the twelve-mile strip of land separating the two rivers, to Fort Donelson, having already ordered Foote to approach the fort (going around by way of the Ohio) and, at the agreed time, take it under fire. After waiting two days for the arrival of a reinforcing division under General Lew Wallace, Grant deployed his army. On the morning of the fourteenth Foote's gunships engaged Fort Donelson, but under circumstances far less favorable than those at Fort Henry. His ships took many hits; some lost their steering and drifted helplessly downriver. At a meeting on Foote's flagship the next morning Foote and Grant concerted their plans—their colloquy interrupted by reports of an attempted Confederate breakout. Grant, arriving on the scene and understanding that the attempt to break out had failed, ordered his force to prepare to attack the enemy. The main thrust of the attack would be from the Union right and led by General Smith.

Within twelve hours Grant was handed a request for terms from the remaining Confederate commander in Fort Donelson, Simon Bolivar Buckner. Grant's response is among the two or three most famous ever returned by an American general.

> Yours of this date proposing Armistice and appointment of Commissioners to settle terms of Capitulation is just received. No terms except immediate and unconditional surrender can be accepted. I propose to move immediately upon your works. I am, sir, very respectfully,
>
> > Your obt. svt.
> > U.S. Grant
> > Brig. Gen.

Buckner capitulated. The strategic significance of Grant's victory was enormous; it forced the evacuation of Nashville and the collapse of the whole Confederate position in west Tennessee. News of Grant's triumph spread immediately—it was the Union's first important victory in the war. Lincoln made him a major general of volunteers.

The Southern defeat now implied a concentration of Southern armies farther south; scattered forces, their actions uncoordinated and invariably defense-minded, could accomplish nothing. P. G. T. Beauregard, sent west by Jefferson Davis, believed he could assemble a powerful new army from elements in the Mississippi Valley and farther west, perhaps even launching a campaign north into Kentucky—Paducah, then Cairo and St. Louis. As it turned out, he and General Albert Sidney Johnston assembled their armies near Corinth, Mississippi, the ranks swollen from Mobile, Pensacola, Columbus, Murfreesboro, and those who had escaped from Donelson. It was an unintegrated assembly of poorly equipped, largely untrained recruits (except for those who had seen action at Donelson); most were serving under commanders even less suited to their tasks than those they commanded. By late March, the army numbered about forty thousand.

Had Grant been allowed to move south immediately after capturing Fort Donelson, following the line of the Tennessee, he might have engaged this raw army successfully and won a decisive victory. He now had at least forty thousand men; Major General Don Carlos Buell commanded thirty-five thousand at Nashville. The junction of their forces could provide an invincible army.

That this did not happen (or did not happen when it might have) was mainly a consequence of the cautiousness of Grant's superior Halleck, and of Halleck's manifest jealousy of Grant's victory at Fort Donelson. Yet another pattern was being established: Grant wanting to exploit tactical successes at once; cautious superiors reluctant to give him his head. Halleck played politics, insisting to the secretary of war, Edwin Stanton, that unless he commanded Buell's army as well as Grant's, it would be unsafe to pursue the Confederates. Meantime he castigated Grant for visiting Nashville without permission (where Grant had simply met with Buell) and for withholding reports of troop strength from Halleck's headquarters. And he wrote McClellan, darkly, that Grant "has resumed his former bad habits."

Stanton told Halleck to file formal charges against Grant, if he had reasons sufficient to sustain such charges. But Halleck did not, and he now acquiesced in Grant's determination to move south, toward the enemy, asking only that Grant move cautiously, and that he not bring on a battle until Buell's army, now beginning its long march west from Nashville, joined him.

By mid-March 1862, Grant's army, or most of it, was encamped at Pittsburg Landing, on the west bank of the Tennessee, about twenty miles northwest of Corinth, Mississippi. The stage was set for the most tragic of Civil War battles, Shiloh.

In Corinth, Mississippi, there were now assembled some forty-five thousand Confederates. Their commander, Albert Sidney Johnston, believed he had to attack the Union force before Grant could be reinforced by Buell's army, marching to join him from Nashville. Grant's force of six divisions (one a few miles north of Pittsburg Landing) was established between the river and Shiloh Church, not quite three miles away to the west. What would become the battle-field lay several hundred feet above the Tennessee, the plateau dropping off very sharply at river's edge.

The Union force was not entrenched. Nor had it really taken proper security precautions, as Grant (as was usual) was fully focused on his own planned attack on Corinth. When Johnston's huge force swept screaming out of the surrounding woods at 6 a.m. on April 6, the army was not prepared for battle. The engagement that followed, a desperate struggle that would consume two days and cause the deaths or injuries of more than twenty-three thousand men, was a chaotic engagement, without form or tactic, strategy or pattern. General Johnston was killed that afternoon. Grant, who had arrived by boat an hour after the fighting began, managed by night-fall to stabilize the Union position, especially after early elements of Buell's force began arriving at dusk.

On the night of April 6 a booming storm brought a ceaseless cold rain, and the dying and wounded of both armies lay where they had fallen, waiting for the warm sunlight of a bleak new day. Grant had sought a dry refuge in a shack that had been taken over as a surgery, but was driven away by the agonized screams of those having limbs amputated. He spent the night wrapped in his great-coat, propped against a tree.

The next day, the fighting resumed, and the Union forces regained the ground lost, inflicting sufficient casualties upon the surviving Southern commander (Beauregard) to convince him to retreat to Corinth.

Survivors' attempts to evoke the character of Shiloh are choked by the frustration of exhausted men powerless to communicate the horror they have just seen and lived. "Death was in the air and bloomed like a poison-plant on every foot of soil," a man wrote, ". . . the light of the sun was obscured by . . . clouds of sulfurous smoke and the ground became moist and slippery with human gore. . . . arms, legs and heads were torn off."

Shiloh was a tactical draw, each side sustaining enormous casualties in executing missions the public only dimly grasped. But the battle was in fact a strategic victory for the Union, a victory that General John Pope's concurrent capture of Island Number Ten, in the Mississippi between Cairo and Memphis, made doubly significant. Memphis soon fell to the North, and Confederate forces never again seriously threatened Union armies in the western theater of operations.

But if the public was slow to grasp the strategic consequence of Shiloh, it understood the magnitude of Union losses, and, inevitably, it fastened on Grant's apparent callousness, his prodigal willingness to sacrifice soldiers for no demonstrable purpose.

Afterward Lincoln defended him stoutly. Inevitably Grant's critics had taken up the rumor that he had been drinking and that he was unfit for command. "I can't spare this man; he fights," Lincoln said. Halleck, however, removed Grant from command, assigned him the meaningless job of second in command (duties unprescribed), and redoubled his criticism, always behind Grant's back, to army colleagues. Had it not been for the intervention of his friend Sherman, who found him despondent and about to leave the army on furlough, Grant would have departed this strange predicament at once.

Under Halleck the huge army moved forward. It used a month to capture Corinth, which, when captured, was discovered to be empty of all enemy soldiers. But Halleck soon restored Grant to his command (the Army of the Tennessee), Grant moved his headquarters to

Memphis, and Halleck was assigned as general in chief of all federal forces, in Washington.

Not long after this restoration to command and Halleck's departure for Washington, Grant was reminded that his duties demanded departmental administration as well as the active leadership of soldiers on campaign. One challenge in particular demanded resolution.

Like Abraham Lincoln, Grant had gone to war on behalf of Union—a Union whole and healthy. Beyond this, his proclamation to the citizens of Paducah had asserted, "I have nothing to do with opinions." Soon, however, black refugees began entering Union lines; the problem was sufficiently worrisome that McClellan had already issued an order—General Order #3—which closed all Union lines to blacks in flight from their former masters. But by then such declarations could have but little effect on the huge tide of former slaves seeking, and needing, shelter, protection, subsistence, and work. Moreover these slaves, if returned to the South, would remain, in effect, enemy auxiliaries. To return them to their masters would be wrong; but it would also be foolish.

Grant entrusted the supervision of all such "contrabands" and the resolution of their needs to John Eaton, chaplain of the Twenty-seventh Ohio: to find and assign them work; to build and manage refugee camps, to arrange their assignments, some of them, to work on plantations now abandoned. By December 1862, Grant also began using blacks as laborers for the army, many in the canal-digging projects he had undertaken around Vicksburg; by the spring of 1863 many were in the army, used at first as guards over Union camps and fortifications, soon on more active service. Brooks Simpson credits Grant's own exposure to slaves in the 1850s as having proved to him that black men would work as hard and as effectively as white men. Grant was coming to realize that the war could not be won without the elimination of slavery. This was an evolution on which he reflected proudly, years later, in a conversation in Berlin with the German chancellor, Otto von Bismarck. The latter had remarked, "You [Grant] had to save the Union just as we had to save Germany." "Not only save the Union, but destroy slavery,"

Grant rejoined. "In the beginning [we fought for the Union] but as soon as slavery fired upon the flag it was felt, we all felt, even those who did not object to slaves, that slavery must be destroyed. We felt that it was a stain to the Union."

Grant was never to retreat from this position. After the war, during Reconstruction, and in the eight years of his presidency, Grant's commitment to the freedom of black Americans—and the hard-won privileges and rights of citizenship that such freedom implied for all Americans—sustained his work to preserve these gains long after most citizens in the North had lost interest in them or had given in to an indulged exasperation with their costs and difficulties.

Grant next turned his attention to Vicksburg, the Confederate stronghold above the Mississippi River. Vicksburg's strategic significance in the western theater was comparable to the Shenandoah Valley's in the East. The latter was the Confederacy's breadbasket, a vital transportation artery and natural axis of advance toward the major cities of the lower Northeast; Vicksburg, a small city on the east bank of the Mississippi, set on a high bluff from which well-laid artillery commanded the Mississippi River, served as a guarantor of safe transit for men and goods from the trans-Mississippi West to the lower South. And it denied Union vessels passage below Vicksburg itself, some two hundred miles south of Memphis.

Grant undertook two campaigns to force Vicksburg's surrender. The first, in the winter of 1862–63, failed. But this was a failure from which Grant both learned and took useful lessons. The second, from April until the city's surrender on July 4 after a long siege, established Grant's reputation as a general of rare strategic vision and the executive abilities necessary to implement the movements of forces, their maintenance, and their employment in battle, which brought victory. It is the outstanding campaign of the Civil War.

The first campaign is quickly described. With an army of about forty thousand Grant advanced south along the line of the Mississippi Central Railroad, establishing a supply depot at Holly Springs; but this depot was quickly captured and destroyed by the rebel general Earl Van Dorn, and when other lines of communication were cut by Nathan Bedford Forrest, Grant decided to cut his losses and retreat back to Tennessee. Meantime he had ordered Sherman to take command of a Union force now assembling at Memphis. But after a tortuous passage, down the Mississippi and Yazoo rivers, Sherman's force was roughly handled by the Confederates defending Vicksburg and retreated as well.

That winter Grant conceived a bold plan that ultimately succeeded. In its originality and execution—and in Grant's unyielding allegiance to his vision despite the skepticism of all who knew something of his intention (including Sherman)—it reminds us of Douglas MacArthur's success, against long odds, at Inchon, in 1950. It was simple. Admiral David Porter would run his fleet south on the Mississippi past the Vicksburg batteries—transports, gunships, auxiliary vessels—and they would meet Grant's army, which would have marched down the west bank of the river to a point well below Vicksburg. Porter would then ferry the army across to the east bank, and Grant would approach Vicksburg from the southeast or east.

Grant also planned a strong feint, north of the city, and a cavalry raid in great force that would sweep south across the interior of Mississippi, destroying railroads, depots, telegraphs, moving quickly from one town to another so that the Confederates would imagine the force to be far larger than it was, and would not accurately predict where it would move next. Grant had learned, on the winter retreat, that his army could subsist on the lands it marched over and could cut itself off from its supplies if necessary. Grant proposed to do this again, and the course of the campaign proved him right.

Porter sailed on April 18 and got safely through. Grant's force moved easily and rapidly away from the river, winning several engagements as it advanced, not north toward Vicksburg but east, toward the capital of Mississippi, Jackson. Here the senior Confederate commander in the western theater, Joseph Johnston, had deployed his small force to defend the city. On May 14 it was driven out, easily, it seemed, by Sherman's and James B. McPherson's men, all its factories and shops were burned, and its railways destroyed. Johnston had urged John C. Pemberton, the commander at Vicksburg, to abandon the city and join him, so that the Confederate army could meet Grant with some hope of victory, but Pemberton refused. He would remain in Vicksburg to the end.

By May 17, having won two major victories at Champion's Hill and Big Black, Grant's army stood before Vicksburg. By now Grant's army comprised some seventy thousand soldiers—which, even with a large detachment sent off to "watch" Johnston, was easily adequate to isolate the city. Several assaults proving unacceptably costly, the army settled down to a siege, and the surrender, by now inevitable, was offered on July 4.

In his *Memoirs* Grant wrote that "the fate of the Confederacy was sealed when Vicksburg fell," and indeed, on July 9, the rebels surrendered Port Hudson (more than two hundred miles south of Vicksburg), their last redoubt on the Mississippi. "The father of waters," said Lincoln, again "flowed unvexed to the sea."

Earlier, in the somber days of late winter, criticism of Grant, much of it ad hominem, had mounted from within the general officer corps, including revived claims of Grant's drunkenness. President Lincoln sent Charles A. Dana, the assistant secretary of war, to investigate, under the cover of a trumped-up administrative mission. He was to study Grant, get a sense of him and how he operated. Grant no doubt saw the visit for what it was and went out of his way to engage Dana, to make him feel a part of the field family he lived with. Dana's response was discerning and positive: he had come to scorn, perhaps, but stayed to praise. Grant, he pronounced, was modest, "most honest," with a rare self-possession. He was also, in perhaps the highest adjective of political praise from an earlier century, *disinterested*—which is to say, consciously devoted to Cause, not Self. He had a remarkable ability to get men to do things, the things he wanted done, as well as they possibly could, and to do so with no yelling, no threatening, no cajoling, no promises. He simply communicated a calm confidence that the mission would be done, and done successfully.

Such men don't know what to do, what to say, when they themselves are praised. Abraham Lincoln was surprised when he received no acknowledgment of the following remarkable letter.

13 July 1863

My Dear General

I do not remember that you and I ever met personally. I write this now as a grateful acknowledgement for the almost inestimable service you have done the country. I wish to say a word further. When you first reached the vicinity of Vicksburg, I thought you should do, what you finally did—march the troops across the neck—run the batteries with the transports, and thus go below; and I never had any faith, except a general hope that you knew better than I, that the Yazoo Pass expedition, and the like, would succeed. When you got below, and took Port Gibson, Grand Gulf, and vicinity, I thought you should go down the river and join Gen. [Nathaniel] Banks, and when you turned Northward East of Big Black, I feared it was a mistake. I now wish to make the personal acknowledgement that you were right, and I was wrong. Yours very truly.

Abraham Lincoln

In October, Grant was given command of the "Military Division of the Mississippi," essentially the entire theater of operations from the Alleghenies to the Mississippi. He moved at once via Indianapolis and Louisville to Chattanooga, where General William S. Rosecrans's army, isolated and besieged after having nearly been overrun at Chickamauga, was rumored to be considering withdrawal. It was, in fact, facing starvation; less than a week's rations were on hand, and the Confederates now occupied all the high ground around the city and controlled all but one of the supply routes into it. Grant fired Rosecrans immediately, replaced him with General George Thomas, and made the long journey, much of it on horseback, over mountain trails at night, into the city.

Within a week, under Grant's direction the supply corridor had been opened up and Sherman's and Joseph Hooker's armies ordered to join the besieged Union force. Grant's impact on his new associates perfectly followed his established pattern: this unimpressive little man walked in, slouching and grubby, saying little, asking a few acute questions, earnestly listening, and then, an observer wrote, "so intelligent were his inquiries, and so pertinent his suggestions that he made a profound impression upon everyone by the quickness of his perception."

The plan Grant developed envisioned an attack by Sherman's corps which would turn the Confederate general Braxton Bragg's army right, on Missionary Ridge. General Hooker's troops would attack Lookout Mountain, capture it, and move against Bragg from his rear. Thomas's divisions would move on the Confederate center after the other attacks had been pressed. As it happened, neither Hooker nor Sherman was wholly successful on November 24, when the attack began, though Hooker did capture Lookout Mountain. The next day Grant ordered Thomas forward with his four divisions abreast, instructing him to capture Confederate positions near the base of Missionary Ridge, there to regroup and await instructions.

The soldiers kept going, however; they carried the heights and caused a headlong Confederate retreat. It was a stunning victory, purchased relatively cheaply. Grant followed up by sending Sherman's corps off to Knoxville to relieve General Ambrose Burnside, then facing Longstreet.

That winter, Grant's Illinois mentor, Elihu Washburne, shepherded a bill through the House that revived the rank of lieutenant general, last held by George Washington. Grant was summoned to the capital for his new commission and promotion—and his assignment as general in chief of all Union forces.

He had left Galena, a quiet civilian walking alongside the volunteer infantry company he had helped organize, only thirty-three months earlier. He was forty-one.

5

Victory

Grant was a thoroughly functional soldier, impatient already with the ceremonial and social demands of his new role as general in chief. The day after his arrival at Willard's Hotel and the joyous tumult that had greeted him in its dining room and at the president's weekly reception, he returned to the White House to accept his commission as lieutenant general. He thanked Lincoln—with whom his rapport was instantaneous and complete—made an awkward if heartfelt response to the president's remarks, and spent the afternoon examining Washington's fortifications. The next day, March 10, he left town for the headquarters of the Army of the Potomac at Brandy Station, about fifty miles southwest of the capital. Those who saw him for the first time didn't exactly know what to make of him—this stumpy, awkward, bashful man—but his triumphs in the West, his reputation as a fighter not a talker, recalled to citizens his modesty and self-possession, his aura of silent abstraction. America has always loved a tongue-tied hero, a Charles Lindbergh, a Lou Gehrig; here was the very incarnation of Act not Talk. Vainglory had not succeeded in the eastern theater; quiet competence and determination must now be given their chance. They had succeeded everywhere else that Grant had led soldiers.

Like Zachary Taylor in Mexico, Grant detested military bureaucracy. He mistrusted what it represented and despised its waste. The panoply of spruce generals and frisking aides that he found at headquarters must surely have confirmed Sherman's counsel: "For God's sake and your country's come out of Washington. . . . I exhort you to come out West."

But Grant understood that he must command from the East, if not from Washington, where his old nemesis Halleck, acquiescent in his new role as chief of staff, now ran army headquarters, then from the field. Grant decided to establish his own headquarters near the Army of the Potomac's and its commanding general, George Meade. He would accompany Meade's army (augmented, a force of 120,000) in the campaign against Lee's 60,000. Grant would issue orders to all Union armies, all of its half-million soldiers, using an efficient telegraph service that represented a major new tactical resource for Civil War generals. He would exercise strategic direction over the whole, Meade's army included. Meade, despite his seniority, was now but one of several army commanders whose cooperation would be necessary to accomplish Grant's plan.

This would prove to be a fair-weather arrangement, made not for efficiency but for purposes obviously political, as an earnest of Grant's respect both for the Army of the Potomac and for its leader—who was, after all, the victor of Gettysburg and by several years Grant's elder. It is sometimes argued that Ulysses Grant had blunt political antennae, that he was immune to political nuance as he was tone deaf. But this is wide of the mark. Grant and Meade would labor, this is surely the right word, to make their arrangement work. Grant was acutely sensitive to Meade's position, given his own history of insults absorbed, disappointments, and slights. He worked at keeping Meade happy, praising him, advancing his name for promotion, confiding his gratitude and admiration for Meade's loyalty. He also knew Meade's temperament, its acid brusqueness and sudden rages. Their relationship is best compared to that of an admiral commanding a flotilla with the captain of the flagship on which both live and work. The captain has freedom of action, but only within the compass of his understanding of the admiral's orders and expectations. And the admiral is always there.

Grant's mission was to achieve military victory over Southern armies, to inflict defeats that would, first, make it impossible for them to reinforce one another, and second, force their surrender. Lee's Army of Northern Virginia was most important and its commander by far the most influential of the Southern generals. Grant was now the maker of grand strategy. His plan to win the war was simple, but in war, as Carl von Clausewitz observed, the simplest things are often those most difficult to achieve.

As soon as they could be made ready, the major Union armies would attack simultaneously. At the same time the flow of enemy matériel, of rations and ammunition, would be everywhere irrupted. In the West, Sherman would attack Joe Johnston's army, forcing it back upon Atlanta, bringing it to battle, eliminating it as a serious force; he would then capture Atlanta, before moving through the Deep South and destroying its capacity to sustain the rebellion. Benjamin Butler, an ambitious political general from Massachusetts, would lead the Army of the James from its base in eastern Virginia toward Richmond and Petersburg, destroying the latter's rail communications with the South and West and helping strangle both the Confederate capital and Lee's army. Franz Sigel, another political general, a German immigrant and Missourian, would advance through the Shenandoah Valley from Martinsburg, West Virginia, destroying its crops and railroads and any army in its way, capture the valley rail center of Staunton, then move east toward Richmond. Finally, General Nathaniel Banks, another politician in uniform, was to mobilize all available soldiers in and around New Orleans and lead them against Mobile, Alabama. Banks's force could then join Sherman for the latter's final campaign in the South—its exact objectives as yet to be determined.

Lee's Army of Northern Virginia occupied positions several miles south of the Rapidan River, a stream easily forded at several points, and running west to east to its juncture, ten miles west of Fredericksburg, with the Rappahannock. This army was tough, confident, battle-hardened. Of Lee, the historian Rick Atkinson's observation of Erwin Rommel seems pertinent: "Like most of history's successful commanders, he had an uncanny ability to dominate the minds of his adversaries." What Rommel would be to the British, and Lord Nelson to the French, Lee was to the Union armies in the East—to everyone, that is, except their new general; Grant was respectful of Lee's ability, but that was all.

To get at the Army of Northern Virginia, Grant would have to traverse an area some ten miles wide by seven miles deep, immediately south of the Rapidan, called the Wilderness. This was a choked and dismal land of second-growth forest, hidden ravines, scrub vegetation. Here General Hooker had come to grief eleven months earlier, leading the Union army to a terrible and demoralizing defeat around Chancellorsville. Lee's army knew this terrain as well as any army could know land it had already defended. His generals and field officers knew the Wilderness well enough to use it, rather than to be intimidated by it.

The campaign was to begin on May 4, 1864. Grant marshaled his forces, scouring the East for additional troops on soft duty away from the army. The Army of the Potomac was to move south, cross the Rapidan, march rapidly through the Wilderness, and engage Lee's army in the open country just beyond. Here Meade's superior numbers and artillery would overwhelm the enemy and perhaps interpose between Lee's army and Richmond—though Lee's army, not the capital, was always the object. Nor did Grant tell anyone (Meade included) of the specific elements of the plan. The army did not know, for example, whether it would cross over the eastern Rapidan fords, aiming to get around Lee's right, or use the western crossings, to outflank the Army of Northern Virginia on its left. They were not the only ones in the dark. Four days before the attack began, Grant received the following letter.

> Not expecting to see you again before the Spring campaign opens, I wish to express, in this way, my entire satisfaction with what you have done up to this time, so far as I understand it. The particulars of your plans I neither know, or seek to know. You are vigilant and self-reliant; and, pleased with this I wish not to obtrude any constraints or restraints upon you. . . . If there is anything wanting which is within my power to give, do not fail to let me know it.

And now with a brave Army, and a just cause, may God
sustain you. Yours very truly. Abraham Lincoln.

From May 4 until June 12, Grant's army and the Army of Northern Virginia were in almost continuous contact, much of it in combat, as bloody, and as desperate, as any in American history. The costs
for each side were appalling. Upon crossing the Rapidan, Grant's
army was immediately engaged by the Confederates. Here, in a night-
marish world of flames, smoke, agony, and death, in which friend and
enemy could scarcely distinguish one from the other, the fighting
continued for more than two days. Lee's army now moved south,
taking up prepared positions at Spotsylvania Court House. Grant followed; the armies fought again, continuously for three more days, at
places with names that have endured—the Bloody Angle, the Mule
Shoe. These names have come to stand for combat in which large
numbers of men on both sides fought with a berserk fury that
seemed to lift them beyond, out of themselves. The pattern was
repeated: Lee moving south, always keeping his army between Grant
and Richmond, finally taking up positions, within the sound of Richmond's church bells, at Cold Harbor, six miles east of the capital.

The armies had fought without surcease. But Union soldiers
now understood that, as Grant had told a journalist at the start of
the campaign, "If you see the President, tell him there will be no
turning back." After the two days' fighting in the Wilderness, veteran soldiers, arriving at a familiar fork on a well-traveled road, had
been astonished to see the heads of their long columns turning not
north, back toward the Rapidan, but south. They cheered. They had
fought desperately, been bloodied, but they were remaining on the
offensive. "I propose," Grant wrote a week later, after the worst of
Spotsylvania, "to fight it out on this line if it takes all summer."

"I regret this assault more than any I have ever ordered," Grant
told his officers, the night of June 3, when the Battle of Cold Harbor
was over. The night before, Union soldiers had sewn nametapes on
the backs of their shirts, so that their corpses could be identified
properly and sent home. Their assault went forward, directly into

the teeth of Confederate fire from impregnable positions, at 4:30 a.m. Seven thousand Union soldiers were killed or wounded in thirty minutes; it was Pickett's charge without the glamour, and the results were just as deadly, as were the prodigies of wasted bravery. It brought the total Union casualties for the campaign to forty thousand. Together, the two armies had suffered more than sixty thousand casualties: killed, wounded, or missing.

Grant had hoped for a breakthrough, but he understood that he now had to take the army south of the James and try to get at Lee's army in a different way. He remained sanguine, exhibiting that quality Sherman admired in him so much: faith in victory—a faith that transcended, apparently, the most ghastly of setbacks. A Union officer called Cold Harbor "not war but murder." But in a letter home a senior Union general wrote that "the popular idea of Grant is . . . very wrong. To sit unconcerned on a log, away from the battlefield whittling—to be a man on horseback or smoking a cigar—seems to exhaust the admiration of the country." The officers inferred that, because Grant gave no visible evidence of rage or compassion, exhilaration or depression, he must not have felt such things as other people do.

As word of the Army of the Potomac's awful casualties made its way north, people began to doubt Grant. No victory had been attained, no rebel force routed; the butcher's bill was ghastly beyond reckoning. Lincoln's secretary of the navy, Gideon Welles, a keen and waspish observer of public men, and who had sourly condescended to Grant from the moment he met him, confided an "awakening apprehension that Grant is not equal to the position assigned to him. . . . The slaughtered thousands of my countrymen who have poured out their rich blood for three months on the soil of Virginia under his generalship can never be atoned for in this world or the next if he . . . proves a failure." The word *butcher* began to be heard, a label that would adhere to him almost as tenaciously as *drunk*; the beginning of a reputation only strengthened by the assumption that Northern demography would enable all losses to be made good, so that more, many more young men might pour out their blood. And if Grant was, supposedly, the best the country could send forward, perhaps the country could not, ultimately, win the war against a determined enemy.

But no general determined to succeed in Virginia in 1864 could have achieved victory without horrific loss. Grant had to attack Southern forces in places and positions of the enemy's selection; the weaponry of the day (as in World War I, in the trenches) everywhere favored the defense, and Union artillery in the Wilderness was usually worthless. Medical technology, such as it was, ensured that most serious wounds would lead to ghastly, lingering deaths.

Grant understood that failure was no option. He infused into the army (in a phrase of Lincoln's, applied to another general in less promising circumstances) his own obdurate sense of purpose, explained again by his friend Sherman as the equivalent of a good Christian's faith in his Lord.

This is the Grant who imposed his will on the army by the quiet fact of his competence and tenacity, qualities that diffused themselves through the army. Silence allied to resolution and competence is a most potent form of military leadership. And its effectiveness grows with each victory it enables. It survives defeats (which come to be seen as temporary setbacks) and is able to endure savage losses.

Grant understood that his predecessors in command in the East had failed not because of inferior tactical brains but because they lacked, simply, will. In every battle and campaign in which Grant commanded there seems to have been some defining moment in which he, however unconsciously, communicated his determination not to back off. Such quiet demonstrations of will reassure wavering men; they stir them, not to action but to determination. Thucydides is reported to have said that "of all manifestations of power, restraint impresses men most." Quiet obduracy in a leader is equally formidable.

One of Meade's staff officers observed, "There is one striking feature about Grant's orders: no matter how hurriedly he may write them in the field, no one ever has the slightest doubt as to their meaning, or ever has to read them over a second time to understand them." Grant had what the English call "clear" brains, and the data, the factors that his mind considered in reaching decisions great and small, seem to have excluded all but what the English military historian Corelli Barnett called "neutral factors of calculation." A calmness of physical disposition, so striking to all who met or watched him, natural or schooled, seemed the physical expression of a calm, clear mind. Here is a passage from the best of Grant's military aides' memoirs and recollections of their chief.

> He soon . . . began to write dispatches, and I arose to go, but resumed my seat as he said, "Sit still." My attention was soon attracted to the manner in which he went to work at his correspondence. At this time, as throughout his later career, he wrote nearly all his documents with his own hand, and seldom dictated to anyone even the most important dispatch. His work was performed swiftly and uninterruptedly, but without any marked display of nervous energy. His thoughts flowed as freely from his mind as the ink from his pen; he was never at a loss for an expression, and seldom interlined a word. . . . When he had completed the despatch, he gathered up the scattered sheets, read them over rapidly, and arranged them in their proper order. Turning to me after a time, he said, "Perhaps you might like to read what I am sending."

The British military historian and strategist J. F. C. Fuller finds in one of Napoléon's letters a description of an ideal general in command of large armies.

> [His] first quality . . . is to have a cool head which receives exact impressions of things, which never gets heated, which never allows itself to be dazzled, or intoxicated, by good or bad news. The successive or simultaneous sensations which he receives in the course of a day must be classified, and must occupy the correct places they merit to fill.

It is perhaps not too much to say that Napoléon could have been describing Grant. It is Grant's singular virtue: that he can collect and, as we would say, "process" information equably, dispassionately, and formulate his plan using the evidence available. The execution of the plan depended, of course, on factors Grant could not always control; but military leadership in wartime was the profession, the calling, for which his character and mind suited him ideally. The environment was very different from what he would learn of leadership in politics, which would solicit the employment of a different set of skills, talents, and temperament.

Fuller also compares Grant with his revered rival, noting that while "Lee could not impose his will on Jefferson Davis," Grant—though without any wish or need to try to impose his will on Lincoln—more or less accomplished the same thing by "his quiet unostentatious self-reliance and common sense."

This is the Grant who sat on camp stools whittling, not far from the battle raging all around, saying very little, only listening and thinking, imposing his will on the armies by the quiet facts of competence and resolution—we will see the thing through—a quality that diffused itself through Northern armies.

Grant was indifferent to danger. His aide Adam Badeau observed: "[Grant] never braved danger unnecessarily; he was not excited by it, but simply indifferent to it. I have often seen him sit erect in his saddle when everyone else instinctively shrank as a shell burst in the neighborhood." "His hand never shook, he did not look up, and continued the dispatch as calmly as if he had been in camp." "Ulysses don't scare worth a damn." There is a less happy inference: anyone so impassive, so indifferent (so it seems) to war's horrors must own the gross gift of an inferior, almost inhuman sensibility. He must be a butcher. How else could he have beaten Lee?

Five generations after the Civil War the vague but common knowledge is that Grant the general *was* a butcher; that he callously sacrificed the lives of soldiers (of which his supply was inexhaustible) in brutal and needless attacks against a gallant enemy.

The common knowledge is wrong, but it is sustained by several factors. One of these is the culture's ennoblement of the commander of the Army of Northern Virginia. Lee's reputation is as a tactical genius, always making do with less. Beyond this he was seen, in both North and South, as an embodiment of nobility, as humbly allegiant to a cause in which he believed deeply, and a cause he had not made his own without the searching of a patriot's soul. He was a paragon of modest stillness, forbearance, and humility, and in his person incarnated the virtues of Washington, indeed of Marcus Aurelius.

This by itself implied the less attractive quality of his opponent. A casual compilation of adjectives describing Grant's appearance provides evidence of a plebeian character: *slouching, rumpled, stooped, sloppy, stubby, grubby, slovenly, dusty, shuffling*—all the superficial indicia of what a contemporary called a pachydermism—exactly the kind of character, ruthless and unfeeling, that it must have taken to subdue General Lee.

The numbers do not support such a verdict. Union casualties in the Wilderness campaign were, it is true, terrible, many the consequence of doomed assaults against well-prepared Confederate positions. The key word is *assaults,* for the Army of the Potomac was the aggressive, not the defending, partner in this deadly, prolonged engagement. Casualties were bound to be severe; neither side had adapted to the changes in weaponry that had recently occurred. In such famous acts as Pickett's charge and the Union charge at Cold Harbor, the attacker was, in fact, doomed. Union losses in many of the battles in the Virginia campaign were larger; but as a percentage of troops engaged, they were in fact smaller than Lee's.

All along, failing the destruction of the Army of Northern Virginia north of the James, Grant had intended to order Meade's army (newspapers by now called it Grant's army) south of the James River, to attack Petersburg and destroy the railways feeding into the city, thence into Richmond, from the south. The army silently disengaged from its positions at Cold Harbor and marched the twenty-five miles to predetermined crossing points. Then, using a pontoon bridge thought a marvel for its day, and a flotilla of naval vessels and commandeered boats, the army crossed over. A vanguard force under Ben Butler's deputy Baldy Smith, had it moved swiftly, could have "walked into Petersburg," but by the time this careful commander considered his force ready to move, it was too late. The Confederate commander, Beauregard, had already occupied Petersburg's defenses. The armies now settled down to static warfare—which, various initiatives on both sides being tried, and failing, would last into the early spring of 1865. Grant established his headquarters at City Point, a high bluff overlooking the James, near its juncture with the Appomattox. From this place he would direct the armies for the rest of the war, its last week excepted.

Union casualties for the campaign to date approached sixty-five thousand; and though the president spoke up loyally and sincerely on Grant's behalf, calling for understanding and patience, many in the North were becoming angry and disillusioned with the famous general. It was not only the casualties but also the sense that Union strategy offered no real hope; and that the general in chief, though he would fight it out on any line for any length of time, was essentially a callous man, inured to the suffering of his soldiers; he was a batterer, deficient in sensibility, bankrupt of strategic ideas.

Lee's army was in defensive positions, mostly in trenches, around Petersburg. Grant's strategy was to hold—fix—the rebels in position and prevent them from reinforcing other Confederate forces, all the while extending his own lines farther south and southwest, sundering Petersburg's links to the South, and exploiting whatever weaknesses could be discovered in Lee's lines around the city.

A simple theory of leadership instructs leaders to hire, and reward, the ablest people they can find, provide them with a mission, coordinate their actions—and leave them alone. Ulysses Grant was, however, constrained in his ability to select or relieve subordinates. He could not hire and fire at will. He had complete faith in Sherman, barely less in Philip Sheridan, but other army commanders had been selected for reasons not always linked to their aptness and fitness for various high commands. Often they could not be fired because of their assumed, sometimes real, political importance. Sigel, for example, though eventually replaced by David Hunter, had proved completely unfit to command the Union force in the Shenandoah; and for his part Hunter, ordered to sever Richmond's rail and canal links with western Virginia, turned back in the face of only moderate resistance, elected to retreat—not down the valley (i.e., north) but west, over the Alleghenies. This uncovered the valley to any initiative Lee chose to make; he was quick to exploit the opportunity, detached Jubal Early with a corps, who marched down the valley and menaced Washington. Not until Grant's assignment of Sheridan as commander in the valley, with orders to destroy all enemy forces and lay waste the valley's resources, and Sheridan's execution of these orders, was the valley safe for the Union.

Farther south, the other main Union initiative now wore, in the French historian Halevy's phrase, "the irrefutable consecration of success." Sherman and his army had taken Atlanta on September 2, following a long and torturous campaign across northwest Georgia, and fought against the Southern general Grant admired most, Joseph Johnston. The capture of Atlanta guaranteed Lincoln's reelection, and Sherman, like Grant a convinced adherent of total war, now began his march of devastation to the sea. Savannah fell on December 21, and with Sherman's march north through the Carolinas, the closing of the last Confederate port on the Atlantic (Wilmington, North Carolina), as well as the destruction of John Bell Hood's army before Nashville—and, finally, the virtual isolation of Richmond from the west—the endgame would now be played out.

On March 29 Grant ordered Sheridan to attack the next morning, to "push around the enemy . . . and get onto his right rear." By April 5 Sheridan had done so, winning an overwhelming tactical victory at Five Forks, some fifteen miles southwest of Petersburg. The last railroad into the city was cut, the lines around Petersburg crumbled, and Lee now notified Jefferson Davis that the army must abandon Richmond and strike out for the West, toward Amelia Court House forty miles away, astride the Richmond and Danville Railway. Here the Army of Northern Virginia could replenish its supplies and, conceivably, make its way to North Carolina, to join Joseph Johnston's army to continue the fight.

But this wan hope was disappointed. Union troops were already astride the railroad south of Amelia, and the supplies delivered to Lee's troops turned out to be not food but small-arms ammunition. The army was forced to march farther west, toward the town of Farmville on the Southside Railroad. Here, possibly, supplies from

Lynchburg might be delivered. But this hope, too, was not to be realized. Lee's army suffered another demoralizing defeat at Sayler's Creek, a few miles east of the town; Lee's effectives were down to fifteen thousand—and these men, to have any chance at resupply, pressed on to Appomattox, farther west still. On April 7 Sheridan told Grant, "If the thing is pressed, I think Lee will surrender." Lincoln had seen the message, forwarded to him by Grant. "Let the thing be pressed," he wired. Late that night Grant told officers with him, "I have a great mind to summon Lee to surrender." He wrote at once, sitting in a hotel in Farmville:

April 7th 1865

Gen R.E. Lee
Comd.g C.S.A.

General,
The result of the last week must convince you of the hopelessness of further resistance on the part of the Army of Northern Va. in this struggle. I feel that it is so and regard it as my duty to shift from myself, the responsibility of any further effusion of blood by asking of you the surrender of that portion of the C.S. Army known as the Army of Northern Va.

Very respectfully
your obt. svt
U.S. Grant
Lt. Gn.

Lee received this letter that night; he showed it to Longstreet, who said, simply, "not yet." Lee sent his response.

I have rec'd your note of this date. Though not entertaining the opinion you express of the hopelessness of further resistance of the Army of N. Va.—I reciprocate your desire to avoid the useless effusion of blood and therefore before considering your proposition, ask the terms you will offer on the condition of its surrender.

Grant responded the next day, April 8, now confident, as he wrote the secretary of war, "of receiving the surrender of Lee and what remains of his Army by to-morrow."

General,
Your note of last evening, in reply to mine of the same date, asking the conditions on which I will accept the surrender of the Army of N. Va., is just received. In reply I would say that *peace* being my great desire there is but one condition I insist upon, namely: that the men and officers surrendered be disqualified for taking up arms again, against the Government of the United States, until properly exchanged.

I will meet you or will designate Officers to meet any officers you may name for the same purpose, at any point agreeable to you, for purpose of arranging definitely the terms upon which the surrender of the Army of N. Va. will be received.

Lee responded that he had not intended to be understood as proposing surrender; rather, to ascertain what terms might be proposed. He could not meet, he wrote, to discuss surrender, only to learn how "[Grant's] proposal may affect the C.S. forces under [Lee's] command, and tend to the restoration of peace." Lee asked for a meeting on this basis.
Grant gave no ground.

Your note of yesterday is received. As I have no authority to treat on the subject of peace, the meeting proposed . . . could lead to no good. I will state however General that I am equally anxious for peace with yourself and the whole North entertains the same feeling. . . . By the South laying down their Arms they will hasten . . .

In the language of an age from which all military chivalry has vanished, Lee was keeping his options open. He was satisfying as well as he could the diverging claims of honor, and of the possible interventions of chance or the unexpected, even the possibility that his

depleted army could mount a successful attack in the hope of sur-
prising and breaking through the force now slowly encircling his
army. But such options vanished for the last time on the morning of
April 9, Palm Sunday, when Brigadier General John B. Gordon's
brigades found, beyond a thin line of Sheridan's advance force that
they had pushed aside, some thirty thousand Union soldiers deployed
and waiting for them. Gordon informed Lee, who answered, "There
is nothing left for me to do but go and see General Grant, and I
would rather die a thousand deaths." There was a perhaps inevitable,
halfhearted suggestion from a staff officer: let the army disperse—
we can fight on as guerrillas. But Lee quietly put the idea to rest. It
could lead only to anarchy.

Many of the details of the famous meeting have entered into
mythic lore of our national history: the disappearance of Grant's
migraine on receipt of Lee's letter of that morning, finally asking for
"an interview in accordance with the offer contained in your letter";
the contrast in appearance of the two leaders—Lee, grand and composed, magnificently accoutred, and Grant, according to a member
of his own staff, "covered with mud and in an old faded uniform,
looking like a fly on the shoulder of beef." Observers and writers
wondered whether this was an artifact of contrivance; they could
not have been further from the truth: Grant had had no access to a
clean uniform, and, ever the functional man and soldier, considered
promptness much more important than appearance. Yet the contrast must have made him somewhat uneasy. They slid into an easy
exchange of reminiscence—of their service in the old army, remembering Mexico. Several Union staff officers entered the parlor of the
McClean House and formed a loose semicircle behind Grant; Lee
was attended by one officer only.

They moved to their business. The essential Grant is revealed in
his recollection, many years later, of how he set down the terms
that he and Lee had agreed on: "When I put my pen to paper I did
not know the first word I should make use of in writing the terms. I
only knew what was in my mind, and I wished to express it clearly
so there could be no mistaking it." This is the Grant who ran
through his preparations at West Point with no deliberate study;

who wrote orders in perfect and coordinated sequence to subordinate commanders, each order pellucid, austere with purpose; whose mind was clear, as we should say, whatever the circumstance.

Lee asked that the agreement proposed be put in writing and Grant did so, and at the end of his summary added the instruction that the sidearms and horses and private baggage of the officers would not be confiscated. "This done, each officer and man will be allowed to return to their homes, not to be disturbed by the United States authority so long as they observe their paroles and in the laws in force where they reside."

The nature of the future of the American polity has on occasion been defined by the actions of a few citizens. In the week before the Appomattox meeting, and on the day itself, April 9, 1865, these two men, by their actions and words, largely determined the character of what would follow four years of civil war, and by their example summoned successors to heed always the counsels of their best selves. It was not only a matter of authority or stature; it was an achievement of communicated sympathy, of magnanimity and understanding on the one hand, and of transcendent courage and farsightedness on the other. Had these two men not been the makers of the surrender, had they not understood and thereafter supported the elements of that surrender, and had Ulysses Grant not served as its guarantor, the consequences for the United States would have been profoundly different. For if Grant was determined to win the war, which meant dissuading Lee and the Army of Northern Virginia from all further resistance, knowing that Lee's surrender would almost surely precipitate the surrender of Southern arms everywhere—if Grant was determined to win the war as rapidly as it could be won, he understood also that the object of the war, ultimately, was not victory but peace, and that the work of reconciliation and reconstruction must now be undertaken (it had already begun) as soon as the surrender occurred.

Grant had met with the president on March 28 on the steamer *River Queen*, and no doubt he was powerfully impressed by Lincoln's insistence that the rebel armies be treated magnanimously following the surrenders that now seemed certain. Lincoln urged generous terms, stressing the need for reconciliation as soon, and as completely, as possible: "They won't take up arms again. Let them go, officers and all. I want submission and no more bloodshed. . . . I want no one punished; treat them liberally all around." Like his hero, Grant must be a principal in this final act. The Appomattox terms were astonishingly magnanimous (as the instrumentality by which a civil war of four years' duration was ended); and they were immediately recognized as such by a Southern commander who not only understood but was prepared to enforce his understanding that to continue the war as a guerrilla campaign would guarantee a future of bitterness and hatred that would poison irretrievably whatever final arrangement might ensue.

This was Ulysses Grant's finest hour, as it was Lee's. For the next twelve years, Grant would labor to fulfill what he took to be Abraham Lincoln's vision for a nation made whole.

6

The Road to the White House

In her memoirs, published some years after Ulysses Grant's death, Julia Grant recalled incidents on the day of Lincoln's assassination, April 14, 1865, encounters that had seemed strange and ominous. At dusk, a grim horseman had turned back to peer into the carriage taking her and Jesse to Union Station for their trip to New Jersey. (General Grant was in another carriage.) Later that night she overheard a scuffle on the platform at Havre de Grace, Maryland, as their train left the station. A brakeman was fighting off an unknown assailant trying to get into the Grants' private car, the same man, presumably, who later wrote Julia an anonymous letter about the incident—grateful, he said, that he had failed in his mission. It is certain that Grant, like Secretary of State William Seward and others, had been a target of the Booth conspiracy. Only the intervention of chance had saved him—or, more particularly, Julia's determination to avoid having to spend the evening in the company of Mary Todd Lincoln at the theater, and her husband's determination to be with her.

She remembered also what Grant said to her, just after he told her in Philadelphia that the president had been assassinated. Julia asked whether this meant Andrew Johnson would immediately succeed him. Yes, Grant answered, and "for some reason I dread the change." As Jean Edward Smith has pointed out, Grant already sensed a vindictive spirit in Johnson, who had complained that the Appomattox terms were too lenient. Grant's magnanimity, like

Lincoln's, was rooted in a sympathetic understanding of a defeated enemy's desperate condition. The last paragraph of Lincoln's second inaugural, "with charity for all," and the president's desire to "let 'em up easy," might well have been his own. Navy secretary and diarist Gideon Welles limned Lincoln at the April 14 cabinet meeting as "full of humanity and gentleness," and in one of his last public statements Lincoln had said that "there was too much disposition, in certain quarters, to hector and dictate to the people of the South, to refuse to recognize them as fellow citizens."

But contempt for magnanimity—"it will be understood as weakness"—had already manifested itself as an important conditioner of the radical Republicans' view of postwar policy and Johnson's response to Lincoln's prospective postwar policy. Stout proponents of Negro suffrage in a reconstructed and cleansed Union, the radicals were at first reassured by what they had heard from Johnson. An Indiana congressman reported attending a caucus the day after the assassination in which "the feeling was nearly universal that the accession of Johnson to the presidency would prove a godsend to the country." The radical Benjamin Wade told the new president, "Johnson, we have faith in you. By the Gods, there will be no trouble now in running the government." And Johnson replied, "Robbery is a crime; rape is a crime; treason is a crime: and a crime must be punished. Treason must be made infamous . . . and traitors must be impoverished."

In the week following the assassination Grant learned the terms of Joseph Johnston's surrender to his friend Sherman, in Raleigh, North Carolina. Sherman had been faithful to the spirit of Lincoln's expressed wishes on the *River Queen*: he and Johnston had made what in effect was a peace treaty between two equals determined to restore concord between North and South. Confederate forces would march home to their respective state capitals, turn in their arms, agree to accept the restored Union, disband as military units, and resume their lives as peaceful citizens of their states— which would simply resume their old places in the Union, current state officials taking the oath of allegiance to the national government. Nothing was said about slavery.

President Johnson and Secretary of War Stanton were aghast. Stanton suggested that Sherman had acted treasonously—and made his reaction known widely. It fell to Grant to visit North Carolina, to invalidate the agreed terms, and to ensure that Sherman offer Johnston the same terms he had given Lee; no more. If Johnston did not accede, fighting would resume. It is likely that Grant briefed Sherman on the sentiments prevailing in the capital, on Stanton's and Johnson's attitudes toward him, and on what they had said when they learned of the agreement. As it turned out, Johnston gave way, Sherman telling Grant he had expected the rejection of the proposed terms. While "a gentle spirit pervaded the spent armies North and South," as the historian Louis Coolidge wrote, a spirit of forbearance based on shared suffering, the aftermath of Lincoln's assassination had brought hysteria and a renewed vengefulness to Washington.

On May 23 Grant joined the president and huge crowds for the two days of a grand review of the victorious armies of the United States. The first day, following their commander, George Meade, the Army of the Potomac passed by; the second, an army of a distinctly different character in rough, worn uniforms and in formations three miles long, and a loose-jointed, loping stride: the Army of the Tennessee, Sherman's westerners, tough, bronzed, lean men. Sherman ostentatiously left them to mount the reviewing stand. He exchanged cordial greetings and embraces with old friends. When he came to Stanton, he refused the latter's hand.

Two weeks later a federal grand jury indicted a number of former senior Confederate generals, including Lee, Longstreet, and Johnston, for treason. Lee had already petitioned the president for amnesty (through Grant); now he sought Grant's assurance that the Appomattox terms would indemnify the officers against any such action. The cabinet considered the issue; Grant and Johnson met privately. Grant told Johnson that under no circumstance could Lee be tried for treason. He had given his word, by the terms of the surrender of the Army of Northern Virginia, that so long as the soldiers did not violate their paroles, they could not be arrested, tried, or prosecuted. Had Lee believed the surrender legally problematic, that a

grand jury might later have the officers tried, he would never have
surrendered his army. These men, Grant asserted, can never be tried.
He pledged to resign if Johnson pressed the issue. Here the matter
ended. A later age may judge Grant's action courageous; for Grant, it
was simply duty.

Sometimes accompanied by their children, Grant and Julia now
took an extended vacation trip through the Northeast and Midwest.
It turned into a kind of triumphal procession. At West Point, Grant
received a book of memoirs from his old chief Winfield Scott,
inscribed "From the oldest general to the greatest." In New York he
was feted, dined, acclaimed, lionized as the man who had saved the
Union. But to the repeated cries of "Speech! Speech!" he returned
only humble bows and a few uncomfortable phrases of gratitude—
masters of ceremonies sometimes explaining, sotto voce, that the
general preferred not to speak. This neither surprised nor, apparently, disappointed the crowds and audiences that seemed to materialize everywhere he went; they were entranced by him. The
taciturnity seemed very much in character. Politicians could talk;
victorious generals had no need to. Some admirers made him gifts of
expensive items of furniture and jewelry, plate, a library, ceremonial
swords, even houses, others contributed to large purses of money.

Grant was now general in chief of an army drastically shrunk in
size, much of it on occupation duty in the South. To all intents and
purposes his relationship with President Johnson was cordial. For
the first few months of his presidency Johnson made and imple-
mented decisions in ways that established a reasonable concord
among his various constituencies. Like Lincoln, he believed Reconstruction to be an executive responsibility; he had seen no need to
call Congress into special session at war's end and after the assassination. The steps he envisioned to bind up the nation's wounds
would be swiftly, quietly executed, in a spirit of ordinary business
efficiently restored; and Johnson insisted that the reintegration of
the South into the American polity be understood as, indeed called,
"Restoration," not "Reconstruction."

But Johnson, as soon became apparent, meant these things in a certain way, and his meaning was lost on his visitors. He had certain fixed aims and fierce prejudices. By treason he meant, most ardently, the wartime activities of the rich and wellborn, owners of plantations, scions of old landed families who had served prominently in the Confederate army and government. He particularly despised the abilities of blacks, those abilities needed to enable an effective participation in the duties of citizenship. He saw them as shiftless, sunk irretrievably in "concubinage." Frederick Douglass led a delegation on a White House visit in 1866 to urge that all black men be given the suffrage. But as soon as the delegation had left, the president said to an aide, "Those sons of bitches! I know that damned Douglass; he's just like any nigger, and he would sooner cut a white man's throat than not!"

In amnesty proclamations in late May 1865, Johnson said nothing of the freedmen, offering pardon to virtually all whites save high-ranking officers and those owning twenty thousand dollars' worth of property. He also charged the provisional governor of North Carolina with calling an election of state delegates to a special convention to frame a new constitution for the state; only amnestied white men who had subscribed an oath to the Union could attend. Soon after, Johnson issued similar proclamations to six other southern states. All must repudiate debts incurred during the rebellion; all must declare their secessions null and void; and all must abolish slavery. In August Johnson sent a revealing telegram to the provisional governor of Mississippi, suggesting he allow blacks the vote if they could prove themselves worth $250 and literate. It was a clever cynicism: doubly embarrassing to the northern states, six of whom still vigorously opposed granting voting rights to black men. No southern states implemented Johnson's suggestion in any case, and few blacks had $250.

From the earliest days of his presidency Johnson understood that the support of Ulysses Grant would be critical to the success of his administration and its policies. Grant was the most popular man in the country. He was revered as its military savior, as the incarnation of such qualities of character as would always be the salvation of the Union. But though they were superficially cordial, their relationship was characterized by wariness on each side. Men like Grant, simple and straight, are a puzzle to men like Johnson; as puzzles, they are mistrusted and watched.

Whatever could bind Grant to Johnson was obviously valuable, but this bonding had to be visible. In late November the president sent him on a mission to report on conditions in the South. The report was itself less important than that Grant be seen as the president's emissary. Johnson no doubt believed that whatever Grant wrote could be massaged in ways favorable to himself.

With three aides Grant made a whirlwind tour—two weeks of hurried visits in Virginia, North Carolina, South Carolina, Georgia, and Tennessee. Grant later wrote that he was struck by the loyalty and friendship evinced by his former enemies. An aide, meeting a southern judge recently released from a federal prison, declared that the imprisonment had "done him good"! The party interviewed civilians, legislators, former officers; they observed freedmen and listened to reports. Grant told Johnson that he was "satisfied that the mass of thinking men in the South accept the present situation of affairs in good faith," but he also argued that the military must remain in the South for the foreseeable future, and that the Freedmen's Bureau, established in March 1865 as an agency of the War Department charged with supervising the relief and rehabilitation of former slaves (and white refugees as well), must also remain as an agency in the construction of a new, functioning, loyal South. Grant's report was later summarized for the radical Massachusetts senator Charles Sumner by the secretary of the navy, Gideon Welles, who recited conclusions that Sumner surely did not want to hear. Politicians of strong partisan convictions are invariably made nervous by the thoughtful testimonials of military men that do not fit their own ideological preconceptions.

The Congress that convened in December 1865 refused to seat representatives elected under the auspices of the conventions called in the former Confederate states. Radicals like Wendell Phillips, Charles Sumner, and Thaddeus Stevens, outraged that Johnson had not insisted on black voting rights in these states, contrived to exclude all southern representatives from Congress; they now created a Joint Committee of Fifteen to superintend all the work of Reconstruction. The House passed a bill to strengthen and extend the life of the Freedmen's Bureau; Johnson promptly vetoed it, as he did a civil rights bill—both, he claimed, being unnecessary and, moreover, unwarranted intrusions of federal upon state authority.

Johnson's response included an initiative to create a new political party, appropriating the name National Union, which the Republicans had used in the 1864 election. The president believed the new party would attract Republican conservatives and moderates opposed to Negro suffrage and other radical positions, but he appears to have overestimated the Democrats' willingness to join in a movement less committed to championing Democratic principles than threatening "Republican unity." A convention was summoned in August 1866, in Philadelphia, and its deliberations, coming on the heels of deadly antiblack rioting in Memphis and New Orleans, were configured to present a political program of fairness, reconciliation, and common sense. Delegates from Massachusetts and South Carolina marched arm-in-arm into the great assembly; a committee of a hundred was elected to bear the convention's statement of principles and recommendations to the president. Among other things, this platform asserted that the Union victory "reserved the equal rights, dignity, and authority of the States perfect and unimpaired"—coded language for allowing the states to treat freedmen as they saw fit without federal intervention. The document concluded with a stately paean to Andrew Johnson, "A Chief Magistrate Worthy of the Nation." Johnson's handlers contrived to place General Grant at the president's immediate right at the White House ceremony of presentation, to sustain the public's sense that Grant remained loyal to the president and, at the very least, acquiescent in Johnson's policies.

Johnson had another idea to help advance the purpose: to make political use of a trip to Chicago, where he had been invited to speak at a dedication commemorating a monument to Stephen A. Douglas. The presidential party would entrain in Washington on a leisurely "swing around the circle," a journey that would take them to New York City and upstate, thence to Buffalo, Cleveland, Chicago, and St. Louis before returning to the capital. The president would make his best public case for the election of a sympathetic Congress in the fall elections.

Again Grant (this time with Admiral David Farragut) was brought along as an attendant lord, the hero of Appomattox and already (as Johnson must have understood) a prospective candidate for the presidency. Brooks Simpson observes that citizens of the day, though eager to see and hear their president, expected essentially ceremonial addresses; presidents did not *campaign*, as we understand the term today. They were also expected to present themselves with a becoming dignity.

Johnson did himself much damage on this trip. Constantly hooted at and jeered, easily baited, he shouted out diatribes filled with imprecation and fire, at one point calling for the hangings of Thaddeus Stevens and Wendell Phillips. Grant was disgusted, and at least once he absented himself from the party. What he was now seeing in Johnson had begun to stir a resistant strain in him; the president's wild harangues, his venomous denunciations of radical Republican opponents, his expressed hatred of blacks now outraged Grant's sense of probity. Could the results of Union victory actually be overturned? Was Johnson really determined to reverse the achievements of Union armies, the cause for which many had given their lives? In the 1850s Grant had been far from an abolitionist, but like Lincoln he had moved slowly toward an understanding that slavery must be eliminated, not merely "put on the road to extinction." Now he was determined to defend what he took to be a sacred legacy of the war.

The elections of 1866 constituted an overwhelming defeat for the Democrats and the president. Clearly Johnson and his advisers had misjudged northern voters' attitudes toward their southern policies: the voters had returned three-to-one Republican majorities in both houses; they won every contested statehouse. The vote was a powerful implicit endorsement of the proposed Fourteenth Amendment and a condemnation not only of the outrages perpetrated against blacks in the South but of the failure of state governments to protect the freedmen. This new Congress would be seated March 4, 1867—the day after the end of the (lame duck) session of the Thirty-ninth Congress—ensuring that Johnson would have no space to revive "presidential" Reconstruction. The Thirty-ninth Congress also passed twenty-three bills, giving District of Columbia freedmen the franchise, guaranteeing tenure of office to presidential appointees (which stipulated that Senate concurrence was required to dismiss civil officers appointed during the current presidential term), and requiring all orders issued to the army to be routed through the general in chief (who himself could not be fired unless the Senate concurred). All these measures passed over presidential vetoes.

Congress also passed, over another veto, the Military Reconstruction Act of 1867, a radical measure that placed military governors, to be appointed by the president, in charge of the five military districts into which the territory of the old Confederacy was now to be divided. In effect the states would have to re-earn, re-prove their existence *as states* in the Union; meantime they would be subject to federal military control. A second Military Reconstruction Act ordered military governors to register all eligible voters (freedmen included), to prepare for state constitutional conventions and to facilitate the ratification of the Fourteenth Amendment by the states.

Grant's sympathies were now moving strongly into the radical camp, driven not so much by long-standing conviction as by a realization that without black suffrage there could be no serious hope for the restoration of political comity in the South. Yet he labored to maintain harmonious relations with the president, understanding that Johnson needed his support, and that Johnson, no longer the author or supervisor of Reconstruction, could still do great damage to the process by which the country healed itself. The two men consulted on the appointment of army generals as district commanders, and so far as the country could see, they adjusted their differing claims and disagreements about the actions of such generals satisfactorily.

But this air of cooperation was becoming illusory. In Louisiana General Sheridan had removed the attorney general and later the

governor of the state and the mayor of New Orleans for their failure to prevent the massacre of blacks there. Johnson insisted that
Grant fire Sheridan for not supporting the existing state government in Louisiana, and he also told the general in chief that he
intended to dismiss Stanton as secretary of war. Grant protested
vigorously, reminding the president of his obligations under the
Tenure of Office Act. It was at this time that Navy Secretary Welles
said to the president that Grant was "going over," to which, according to Welles, Johnson responded, "Yes, I am aware of it. I have no
doubt that most of these offensive measures have emanated from
the War Department." Johnson, that is to say, saw in Stanton his
most implacable cabinet enemy, the author of the advice that had
become the legislation that now thwarted him at every turn. Stanton was as radical as Sumner or Stevens; and now he was seen as
carrying Grant with him.

Johnson demanded Stanton's resignation; when Stanton refused,
Johnson suspended him in August 1867 and made Grant secretary
of war ad interim, the latter accepting the position, most likely, to
ensure that it not be given to someone more sympathetic to Johnson's views. Three months later, Johnson believed he had achieved
an understanding with Grant as to the latter's response should the
Senate reverse Johnson's decision to suspend Stanton, according to
the provisions of the Tenure of Office Act. In January 1868, a Senate committee disallowed the president's explanation for the dismissal and prepared to send its recommendation forward to the full
Senate. Grant visited the president and confided his concern: a fine
and a prison sentence if he participated in an effort to retain the
secretaryship illegally. Johnson blustered that this should worry
neither of them—that in fact he would pay the fine or do the time
himself. The two men agreed, so Johnson would later argue, to
resume their conversation after the weekend.

What followed provoked great controversy. Without further
conversation with the president Grant gave the key to the secretary
of war's office to the adjutant general; he returned to his office as
general in chief. He now informed the president by messenger that
he had stood down from his assigned duties as secretary of war ad

interim in order to oblige the Senate's decision. He was no longer secretary, he argued, because his duties had terminated "from the moment of receipt" of the Senate's action.

At the cabinet meeting the next day (Grant having been asked to attend, though he believed himself no longer secretary), the president attacked him for his underhanded behavior in breaking what Johnson understood to be a promise to continue as secretary. Grant denied any such understanding and later sent a letter (made much more forcible by his fierce friend Rawlins) to the president, vigorously denying the allegation against him. Stanton continued to hold the office until Johnson again dismissed him in favor of the army's adjutant general, Lorenzo Thomas. For this action, Congress began impeachment proceedings against Andrew Johnson, a process that would come within one vote of removing Johnson from office.

By this time, the common presumption was that Grant would be the Republican nominee for president in 1868, particularly following the local elections in 1867 that had gone badly for the Republicans and had served to persuade (if not convince) radicals that electability must be the overriding consideration in the selection of a candidate for the following year. National enthusiasm for Grant seemed overwhelming. The *Chicago Tribune* editorialized on Grant's peculiar fitness for the job: "For the President's chief duty is to see that the laws are faithfully executed. Who better is fitted for this than a military man? The training of a military man is that which of all others fits him for executive duty." Still, Grant betrayed no desire for the office. A few months later he wrote Sherman: "[I was] forced into it in spite of myself. Backing down would leave the election to be contested between *mere trading politicians*, the elevation of whom, no matter which party won, would lose us, largely, the results of the costly war which we have just gone through." Such a statement repays study as the embodiment of Grant's view of politics and the kinds of men drawn to its practice and of his determination to protect the achievements of the war as he understood them. The Grant who would not fail the freedman, new citizen and voter, was the Grant of such convictions.

John A. Logan, who as an Illinois congressman had presented Colonel Ulysses Grant to the Twenty-first Illinois only seven summers earlier, placed Grant's name in nomination at the National Union Republican convention on May 20, 1868, in Chicago—less than a week after Andrew Johnson had escaped removal from office by a single vote. Logan's speech evoked wild enthusiasm, and Grant was chosen by acclamation on the first ballot. His running mate, selected on the sixth ballot, was Speaker of the House Schuyler Colfax, described by a spectator as a "good-tempered, chirping . . . real canary bird." Overhanging the dais was a huge portrait of Grant, bearing the taunting label: "MATCH HIM."

The platform supported congressional Reconstruction. It demanded "equal suffrage to all loyal men at the South," while demurely acknowledging that the states themselves should act on this controverted issue—several northern states being among those continuing to withhold the franchise from blacks. The platform further pilloried Andrew Johnson as a tyrant "who has perverted the public patronage into an engine of wholesale corruption," and, in five separate planks, it committed the nominee to reduce taxation, shrink the national debt, and promote "strictest economy" in government.

Grant himself had remained at army headquarters in Washington. He learned of his nomination from the secretary of war, who rushed breathlessly into Grant's office and declared, "General, I have come to tell you that you have been nominated by the Republican party for President of the United States." Grant's first public response, returned in acknowledgment to a crowd that had followed the marine band to his house, manifested the characteristic of most of his public utterances: an earnest sincerity that declared itself in the slightly awkward phrases that the speaker imagined suitable to the occasion.

Gentlemen, being entirely unaccustomed to public speaking and without the desire to cultivate the power, it is impossible for me to find appropriate language to thank you for the demonstration. All I can say is, that to whatever position I may be called by your will, I shall endeavor to discharge its duties with fidelity and honesty of purpose. Of my rectitude in the performance of public duties you will have to judge for yourselves by the record before you.

A few days later, in response to the convention's formal tender of its nomination, Grant signified his acceptance in a sentence that reverberated powerfully everywhere: *"Let us have peace."* However bland, it was understood at first hearing as a heartfelt expression of the nation's most cherished wish. But like the candidate himself, like so many of his actions and utterances, and silences, the statement was soon freighted with a thousand differing translations. What, precisely, did he mean?

The Democrats assembled July 4 in the new Tammany Hall in New York City, nominating the governor of New York, Horatio Seymour, for president, and Francis P. Blair of Missouri as his running mate. Seymour, "the great decliner," had neither sought nor wanted to accept the nomination and was remembered for having addressed the New York City antidraft rioters in 1863 as "my friends." In one of the more vicious caricatures in cartoonist Thomas Nast's portfolio, he was depicted, New York in flames behind him, his side locks twisted into devil's horns, before the rioters, while General Grant—strong, calm, honorable—stands over the detritus of Confederate war making. The caption proclaims, "MATCHED!"

The candidate did not campaign. Rather, Grant and Julia indulged their favorite recreation, traveling. They visited New York, West Point (where their son Fred was beginning his second year), and St. Louis, where Sherman joined them. Without Julia, Grant, Sherman, and Sheridan went far out on the Great Plains to visit Denver, Council Bluffs, and Chicago, Grant declining all invitations to "speak" and Sherman declining his friend's handlers' request for a formal endorsement. When the excursion ended, the family returned to Galena to await the results of the election. John Rawlins was instructed to look after things at army headquarters in Washington. Meantime the campaign went forward vigorously, huge sums of money being raised from prominent eastern capitalists, much of it used to hire correspondents, speakers, and even for the purchase of newspapers. Hundreds of Grant "tanneries" were established; assemblies of veterans marched in nighttime parades; campaign biographies were hurried into print. Horace Greeley's *New York Tribune* ran the following unfortunate doggerel on its front page every day until the election.

> *So boys a final bumper*
>   *While we all in chorus chant—*
> *"For next President we nominate*
>   *Our own Ulysses Grant!"*
> *And if asked what state he hails from*
>   *This our sole reply shall be,*
> *"From Appomattox Court House,*
>   *with its famous apple tree."*
> *For 'twas there to our Ulysses*
>   *That Lee gave up the fight.*
> *Now boys, "To Grant for President*
>   *And God defend the right!"*

Elections in the nineteenth century were held on staggered dates, beginning in early autumn. Voting tendencies could be identified early and easily; momentum in concurrent presidential campaigns could be inferred from these. Republican victories in such early polls now heartened the national campaign. Vermont, in September, went strongly for the Republicans; Maine, Ohio, and Pennsylvania followed. In despair, two important Democratic newspapers urged that the Seymour-Blair ticket be replaced, but it was too late for such radical surgery. As Republicans confidently expected, and as Democratic leaders sensed, the result could not be in doubt. A national hero of unassailable rectitude, his only known flaw one likely to appeal to voters rather than repel them, a man of modest demeanor and blessed taciturnity, of calm competence—the most important and successful military leader since George Washington, and who had proclaimed that he would "have no policy to enforce against the will of the people"—could not, in 1868, be beaten. If Washington had been the father of his country, Ulysses Grant was its savior.

Grant's electoral margin was 214 to 80; he had carried twenty-six states to Seymour's eight; and though his popular margin was only 300,000 (400,000 blacks had voted for him, delivering victories in six southern states), he would have won in the electoral college even without the black vote in the South.

The candidate voted in Galena, declining, however, to cast a presidential ballot. He then retired to Elihu Washburne's house, where a telegraph had been installed. Contemporary testimonials to his calmness, his peculiar lack of excitement at the news he had been elected president, only garnished his reputation for modesty and dutifulness. Before turning in, he spoke to a small band of supporters outside his own house: "The responsibilities of the position I feel, but accept them without fear."

7

Politics High and Low

No president-elect up to 1868 had excited more fevered or hopeful speculation, or more intense scrutiny, than Ulysses Grant. This speculation was overwhelmingly confident in virtually all quarters: from the South, where his magnanimity at Appomattox was gratefully remembered, and where Grant, so far from being seen as a strutting Yankee abolitionist with an itch for money, was understood, in certain ways, to be rather like "one of us"; from the Midwest, certainly, and for the obvious reasons; and from Boston, the Republic's Athens, from the worlds of intellect, pedagogy, punditry, and letters. Henry Adams was almost as effusive in praise of the president-elect as he would later be disillusioned by the president.

For Grant seemed, given the state of things, perfectly apt for the place, the need, the time. One could scarcely use the verb *radiate* in describing the aura of calm self-possession and competence that distinguished him—his was not a radiant presence. He would be the youngest president ever inaugurated (forty-six), and yet he had for so long been a cynosure of national confidence and hope. His record of service was transcendently honorable and victorious; like Emerson's Lincoln, he was a native, aboriginal American. He had borne himself with admirable steadiness through the tortured Johnson years, like the Old Testament king who followed closely in the footsteps of his forefather, swerving neither to the right nor to the left. He seemed both safe and wise—prudent, a man of civic wisdom.

His countrymen also saw in him a settled quality that the historian William Hesseltine called the habit of mute persistence.

Imputation of motive is irresistibly provoked by the silent and self-contained. "That countenance of his never betrayed him," Mark Twain was to write years later. Nor did his activities, or words, in the preinaugural months. Grant was Grant not out of artifice; this is the way, all now agreed, he really was: immune to the blandishments of fame and public approval, he felt no compulsion to explain himself or justify his positions, to the extent that his positions were even known. At his core remained an unanalyzable opacity.

The leaders of the Republican party soon began to fret over Grant's failure to consult them as to cabinet and other senior appointments. A moment's consideration would have reminded them that this was how Grant operated; it was the whole history of his method and mystique. In February, not long before Inauguration Day, Senator Oliver P. Morton of Indiana led a congressional delegation to tender Grant his certificate of election. The president-elect used the occasion to make remarks about appointing people to the cabinet.

> I have always felt that it would be rather indelicate to announce or even consult with the gentlemen who I thought of inviting to positions in my Cabinet. . . . I have come to the conclusion that there is not a man in the country who could be invited to a place in the Cabinet without the friends of some other gentleman making an effort to secure the position. . . . If announced in advance, efforts would be made to change my determination; and, therefore, I have come to the conclusion not to announce whom I am going to invite to seats in the Cabinet until I send their names to the Senate for confirmation.

That is to say, the soldier, whose courage in war was of a quality beyond courage as it is ordinarily understood, faltered before the possibility of causing anger in a colleague. Perhaps this was what Grant had meant, years earlier, when he acknowledged he "had not

the moral courage" to challenge orders or to advance his own arguments. In American politics, then as now, shrinking from saying
things that others may not like is at the root of no end of trouble.

James Russell Lowell wrote, "New occasions teach new duties; time
makes ancient good uncouth." Thus inaugural addresses are expected
to be freighted with bright paeans to the new duties to be asked of
the country. Signs and portents are eagerly sought for, and for once
the wearisome counsel of cynics is unheeded. Listening is in dead
earnest. No hints had been provided; no advance copies of Grant's
inaugural address—which, like all of his speeches, most of his letters,
and large sections of his messages to Congress, he wrote himself.
    March 4, 1869, was a sullen, chilly, and gray day, but from an
early hour parade units had begun gathering, a wild array of distinc-
tive uniforms and military units; clubs representing the various
unassimilated ethnicities of the Northeast, Boys in Blue, Zouaves,
huge bands. Grant and Andrew Johnson did not ride to the Capitol
together; in fact, Johnson did not even attend the inauguration. He
and his cabinet remained together working at the White House until
about the time the oath was being administered. Grant despised
Johnson, and Johnson hated Grant, whom he believed to be a liar.
Instead, shortly before noon, Grant and John Rawlins left army
headquarters for the Senate chamber, to attend to the inaugural
remarks and swearing in of Schuyler Colfax. They then joined the
chief justice, Salmon Chase, on a raised platform at the east front of
the Capitol for the administration of the oath of office. A large
crowd, more than ten thousand, applauded the ceremony, which
was followed by an artillery salute, and by the president's address.

According to Aristotle, rhetoric succeeds when there is a bond of
trust between speaker and audience. That trust is more important
than eloquence—or the absence of eloquence; and it has no necessary connection with it. An honest, competent person laboring to
communicate his own convictions is far more persuasive than a
fluent declaimer whose character the audience may have doubts
about. Grant's speech, only twelve hundred words, was so transpar-

ently the labored effort of a man trying his best to say what he believes, and what he hopes to accomplish as president, that it succeeded powerfully. Listeners were moved and reassured; journalists writing the next day found its messages praiseworthy. It set forth those things important to Grant: the healing commonality of all American citizens—their membership in the restored American nation, a membership not to be defined by race or region, and in which the defining act of citizenship must be voting. The suffrage must be made the right of all; Grant called for quick ratification of the Fifteenth Amendment, which had already passed the House and Senate with the required two-thirds majority and had been submitted to the states to be ratified. Like Abraham Lincoln, Grant had moved a very long way in his last few years in embracing the idea that blacks should have the right to vote.

He argued for the strictest economy in government and the payment of the nation's debt, in gold, as soon as practicable. And he declared, with true feeling, that the country must no longer evade its obligation to "the original occupants of this land"—the American Indians.

It was noticed that, just as Grant began his speech, a bright early spring sun burst through the gloom. Julia Grant later remembered the moment the address ended:

> He stood for a moment, then bowed his acknowledgement to the wild huzzas of the great throng gathered around . . . then he turned and hastening towards me, he stooped and kissed me on the cheek and, with a pleasant smile, handed me his first inaugural address.

Though Grant had sought no counsel as to the substance of his inaugural speech, the message seemed perfectly pitched to the character and culture of this occasion. He reminded his countrymen that the presidential office had come to him unsought and that he "commence[d] its duties untrammeled." A new freedom of presidential action was thus implied, a happy opportunity to paint boldly on an empty canvas.

For all the lofty rhetoric Grant nonetheless understood the political circumstances in which he had been elected, and within which he would have to work. He knew that, even in defeat, the Democrats had attracted a small majority of the white vote; that they had actually increased their representation in the House by more than a third; that a significant minority of blacks had voted Democratic in two southern states; and that huge numbers of immigrants were arriving each month, most settling in the big eastern cities, where they would soon be enlisted as prospective Democratic voters.

To shore up the Republican support, the new president preoccupied himself with matters of patronage and appointment. Just before the inaugural he wrote his sister Mary Grant Cramer: "I scarcely get one moment alone. Office-seeking in this country, I regret to say, is getting to be one of the industries of the age. It gives me no peace." Not only had the whole process (such as it was) of selecting cabinet members and getting them to accept their appointments both surprised and vexed him (it was not like appointing brigadier generals), office seekers jammed his offices and those of his White House staff, most of whom were trusted aides from army days now assigned to the new general in chief (Sherman) but placed on detached duty to serve in the White House. They included Horace Porter, Orville Babcock, and his brother-in-law Frederick Dent, as well as Cyrus Comstock, Adam Badeau, and Robert Martin Douglas, a son of Stephen A. Douglas. The staff gave a military inflection to the operation of the executive mansion, and yet no member seemed to be a martinet or militarist in bearing or ambition. Nonetheless, appointments like these, not first discussed with party leaders, had irritated many members of the House and Senate, because they served notice that Grant was determined to surround himself with the men he wanted; he had not called for nor expected the counsel of legislators.

The politicians, in Hesseltine's tart characterization, were therefore lying in wait to discipline the new president. Their instrument of chastisement was to be the Tenure of Office Act, which had made it impossible for President Johnson to dismiss cabinet officers (such as Stanton). Republican leaders in the Senate, for the most part friendly to the president, were nonetheless chary of giving up a remedy that might prove useful in the future. Just before the inauguration, therefore, the Senate had voted against the repeal of the act. Immediately after, the House having voted strongly in favor of repeal, the Senate refused again to gratify the president. Grant responded in a manner suggested in his inaugural: by a vigorous, by-the-letter enforcement of the Tenure of Office Act. He would remove no Johnson holdovers in any positions, thus rendering congressional patronage (postmasterships, customs officials, etc.) a dead letter. A compromise was soon arranged: the president would be permitted to remove executive appointments with the Senate's approval—"or by the appointment of a successor whom the Senate would accept"—but Grant would be able to hire and fire cabinet members at will. So would his successors.

This compromise disappointed and disillusioned Grant's most idealistic supporters, who saw in it a cave-in to congressional pressure. They had expected a clarion summons to the best and most disinterested citizens, such men who would serve as long as the president desired. Charles Eliot Norton in Boston noted sadly that Grant's "surrender to the politicians is an unexpected disappointment." Critics did not fail to notice, either, the ineptitude of Grant's method. He had not done the necessary political things—the same kinds of activities for which his generalship had been subject to criticism: he had not prepared his ground, or made a careful reconnaissance, or undertaken a detailed study of his enemies. It was at this early time, also, that Grant's own use of patronage began to excite unfavorable comment—most egregiously, his appointment of his father to the postmastership of Covington, Kentucky, and his acquiescence of several of his father's additional recommendations.

The president's cabinet appointments, sprung on the Congress immediately after the inauguration, did not go down well—though the press saluted them as men appointed not for seamy political affiliations and purposes but for merit and for the settled habit of rendering objective advice. The Senate was particularly offended that Grant had not solicited members' advice; and Republican leaders that Grant had made no effort to honor or reward men it thought deserving. Charles Sumner, the Massachusetts radical and chairman of the Senate Foreign Relations Committee, was especially offended at not having been consulted as to the new secretary of state; he may well have wanted the post for himself. (From the beginning Grant and Sumner disliked each other. Sumner, it may be said, represented a type with whom Grant's relations would always be uneasy: the cultivated, verbal, widely lettered, wellborn New Englander.)

For the most part the president seemed to have appointed men congenial to himself, men who (for reasons not made plain) struck him as suited to the portfolios they would assume. Several appointees were men the president barely knew. The cabinet of Grant's day was small—seven members only—and the criticism that they had been chosen and appointed, and would be used, as so many military-style staff officers was soon heard. Grant would, in other words, delegate to the able and attend to his own business.

To his old friend and mentor Elihu Washburne, Grant offered the position of secretary of state, the understanding being that Washburne would serve in this post for two weeks only and then take up an appointment as minister to France—but with the enhanced prestige of having been secretary of state. Contemporary Washington reacted with shock and amusement: Washburne, it expected, was deserving of some cabinet post, but surely not secretary of state! As soon as he did submit his resignation, Grant offered the post to Hamilton Fish, a Hudson River grandee with a distinguished career behind him, as governor of New York and senator—and, for many years, as chairman of the board of Columbia University. Fish was astonished to receive Grant's telegram out of the blue. The wire struck him (however flattering) as peremptory beyond belief, an act as casual as selecting a gardener.

He begged off, citing his wife's ill health. But Grant persisted, assuring Fish that he could be excused after the current congressional session ended. He sent forward Fish's name without having heard back from him.

As it happened, Fish became a superb secretary of state, serving in the cabinet until the end of Grant's second term. The great political historian Richard Hofstadter, assessing his service as secretary, called him a "man of conspicuous rectitude who adorned the group like a jewel in the head of a toad." He was Grant's constant counselor, an early example of an eastern establishmentarian perfectly comfortable serving a president of profoundly different provenance.

The new president had thought to reward his loyal chief of staff Rawlins with an appointment as commander of the military department of the Southwest, but Rawlins wanted more, and Grant obliged his dear friend by making him secretary of war.

For secretary of the navy, Grant made a bizarre choice, Adolph E. Borie, a wealthy Philadelphian and society lion who had contributed to Grant testimonials and who was becoming something of a crony. Borie was an accumulator of wealth, "and at that time General Grant placed a high estimate upon the presence of talents by which men acquire wealth," according to a later treasury secretary. The mutual attraction of the wealthy and the political (and military) is one of ancient and continuing vitality in American history. For his part, Borie was astonished to be tapped for the post, as he knew nothing of the navy or government. His was precisely the situation of the rising Tory MP who, when asked to be chancellor of the exchequer, confessed that he knew nothing of finance. "It's all right," came the response. "Mr. Canning didn't either. They give you the figures."

Borie took up the unfamiliar burdens of his nautical responsibility with the understanding that he would be allowed to withdraw as soon as he could do so gracefully. He did.

Grant's other cabinet appointments included John A. Cresswell of Maryland, a war Democrat turned radical, a U.S. senator, and an early supporter of Grant's nomination in 1868. Grant made him postmaster general—the principal patronage officer, after the president and congressional leader, in the country. He was an administrator of unusual aptitude and steadiness, and his work was universally applauded. Grant appointed Ebenezer Rockwood Hoar, of Massachusetts, as attorney general. An associate justice of the Supreme Judicial Court of his native state, he was widely regarded as an accomplished and wise lawyer and man of letters. For secretary of the interior, he selected General Jacob D. Cox of Ohio, whose name had been suggested to Andrew Johnson during the Tenure of Office crisis as a possible permanent successor to Edwin Stanton. He was a professor of law in Cincinnati and had not been informed that he was under serious consideration for this or any other post in the administration.

Finally, Grant nominated Alexander T. Stewart to be secretary of the Treasury. He was the richest retail merchant in the world and, like Borie, a major contributor to Grant's homes and to Republican causes generally. No doubt Stewart, who wanted the position, would have served ably. But it was not to be; senators had discovered a relatively obscure statute, dated 1789, that forbade the treasury secretaryship to be filled by anyone in trade. Grant immediately sought a waiver, and though it cleared the House easily, senators of both parties were quick to insist the appointment was not appropriate. For his replacement, Grant selected George S. Boutwell, a Massachusetts radical Republican who had served on the committee that brought impeachment charges against Andrew Johnson.

For none of these appointees was there anything remotely approaching a "vetting process." Grant appointed men to his cabinet as he had appointed them to his military staffs, trusting his judgment, his sense of who would be the most serviceable and loyal—and manageable—colleagues. No serious contemporary student of Grant, in or out of government, had any reason to expect that he would have made such appointments in any other way. And as it happened, the cabinet as a whole proved to be an able one, somewhat above the average, all members taken together, in substance and ability, from most cabinets of the long Indian summer of American politics, between Abraham Lincoln and Theodore Roosevelt.

The new administration at once showed its determination to address the nation's equivocal financial condition. The national debt was nearing three billion dollars. (At the start of the Civil War it had stood at sixty-four million dollars.) "The payment of principal and interest," as Grant had insisted in his speech, "as well as a return to a specie basis, as soon as it can be accomplished without material detriment to the debtor class, must be provided for." He insisted all national indebtedness be discharged by gold; the Congress, just two weeks after Inauguration Day, accommodated him in the Public

Credit Act, which committed the country to pay all its bondholders in gold and to begin at once to redeem greenbacks, the paper currency issued to help finance the war, some $376 million of which remained in circulation. Boutwell, a "safe" if unimaginative treasury secretary, radical in his Reconstruction politics but as conservative as the president fiscally, set to work immediately to reduce the debt. He bought bonds and sold gold, committing the proceeds to the sinking fund, reassuring bankers, and, coincidentally, gradually reducing the size of interest payments on various bonds. He fired a number of Treasury Department employees and drastically increased the efficiency of government collections of duties and taxes. What Boutwell could not have foreseen was that a complex skein of events would be set in motion early in the summer of 1869, driven by the ambitious greed of Jay Gould and Jim Fisk, two friends of Abel Rathbone Corbin, the president's new brother-in-law.

The sixty-one-year-old Corbin had recently married the president's favorite sister, Jenny. Corbin was a business operative and manipulator of a type familiar in the postwar years, a promoter, influence monger, and part-time lobbyist. Gould, a young man who had already realized a spectacular success with the Erie Railroad, and Fisk, who had made a fortune in Civil War smuggling, determined to enlist the president's new brother-in-law in a scheme to manipulate and quickly corner the gold market. Fisk and Gould believed, also, that the president himself would have to be brought to an implicit acquiescence in the plan, with Corbin functioning as an apparently innocent go-between. The president was known to be especially devoted to Jenny (he had given her away at the wedding) and very close to Corbin, whom he had known for many years.

The successful corner depended on the conspirators' knowledge of how the administration's policy with regard to the sale of gold operated: that is, how much gold the government would auction off in New York each week, if any. Since very little gold was in actual circulation, such auctions had an immediate, potent impact on the price. The more gold that was sold, the lower the price. Gould's stratagem was to argue that gold at its current price ($135 per ounce) was too "cheap" to attract European buyers. If the price could be moved to, say, $145 per ounce, such prospective buyers would be powerfully drawn to participating in the American market. They could get more crop for their money, and the American farmer would be the immediate beneficiary. Either government policy had to be controlled, manipulated somehow, or the conspirators had to find out the Treasury Department's auction plans in advance: how much gold, if any, was to be sold each week.

This much Gould told Corbin. The men also took a run at Assistant Treasury Secretary Daniel Butterfield, who was directly responsible for the New York gold sales. Gould gave him ten thousand dollars for his prospective help; and he offered Grant's White House aide Horace Porter a much larger sum, though Porter turned him down.

Fisk was a preposterous figure, a kind of caricature of what he believed the world would admire and envy. Ostentatious, self-indulgent, promiscuous (he would be gunned down, many years later, by the husband of a woman he was seeing), a militia "colonel" in the war, and, by his own authority, admiral of a steamship line. While Corbin was to "share" the conspirators' novel theory of crop movement and their devotion to the interest of the American farmer, Gould and Fisk would contrive to attend dinners or receptions at which the president would be present—on one occasion, not long after Grant began his summer holiday, conveying him on Fisk's Bristol Line overnight steamer from New York to Boston. After dinner Fisk asked the president, straight-out, to describe for him his views of gold policy. Grant demurred, noting that for him to do so "wouldn't be fair." (Years later Grant told a correspondent, "I should have felt insulted by such a proposal had it come from any other person like Fisk. But coming from a man so destitute of moral character, I didn't think it worth noticing." One might ask whether, if this were so, Grant should have placed himself in the company of such a man.)

Gould's purchases had been insufficient to drive the price significantly, but he quieted Fisk's qualms, according to later testimony, by assuring him that the "matter is all fixed up; Butterfield is all right; Corbin has got Butterfield all right; and Corbin got Grant fixed all right." By August 25, even a *New York Times* editorial seemed to have sniffed out the conspirators' scheme: "It is not likely Treasury gold will be sold for currency to be locked up." A rise in the price of gold could safely be assumed. In other words, the conspirators had convinced themselves that they had "gotten through to the President."

The Grants stayed with the Corbins for three days in mid-September, the price of gold edging modestly forward as Gould and Fisk steadily, although not dramatically, increased their holdings. Notwithstanding, after the Grants had left for the mountain retreat of Julia Grant's cousins in western Pennsylvania, a worried Corbin sent a messenger with specific instructions to deliver a confidential letter to Grant, and to wait for a reply. It appears that Gould ordered this action—the letter presumably stressing Gould's argument for keeping gold off the market—to help with crop movements. Corbin instructed the messenger to telegraph the president's reply.

The scene wears the aspect of Edwardian farce: The harried messenger exhausted and soiled from his sleepless overnight trip from the city; the president of the United States and his handsome aide Porter (a son of the former governor of Pennsylvania) playing croquet; the president suddenly excusing himself to read the letter, and returning, promptly, with the answer "All right." The messenger, assuming the meaning was that the message had been safely delivered, then sent a telegram to Corbin: *Letter Delivered. All Right.* The recipient, assuming the meaning to be that the message had been understood and that everything was all right, informed Fisk, who now began to buy up gold at a heavy pace—heavy, if well disguised. For his part, the president, still in Pennsylvania, by now fully on the qui vive, instructed Julia to write Jenny Corbin and have her husband cease his activities, whatever they were, at once. When Corbin heard this, he informed Gould, for whom everything suddenly came into focus.

Gould began selling gold the next day (Thursday, September 23), all the while making smaller purchases to gull the market, while his estranged co-conspirators continued to buy. By late morning of what would soon be known as "Black Friday," September 24, 1869, the price of gold touched 163½. And here it trembled, tottered, wavered, and began to plummet as word spread (like wildfire) that the secretary of the Treasury, on orders from U. S. Grant, was selling four million dollars' worth of gold at auction that day.

Actually Boutwell had argued for a smaller amount, but Grant overruled him. As it happened, Abel Corbin and Jenny were guests at the White House for Sunday dinner, two days later, and Corbin again offered his friend unsolicited advice: reconsider the "sell" order and rescind it. Grant refused.

Though the government had intervened in what Jean Edward Smith calls a "watershed" action in the history of American finance, the effects of Black Friday were profound. There was a precipitous decline in the stock market; within a week trading was halved, and traders were ruined. Whether Gould ever reflected on the irony of the farmers' losses—considering he had argued that increasing the price of gold would "help move the crops"—is not known. He and Fisk hired the best lawyers available and beat the rap.

There is little evidence that the Black Friday episode served to put the president on his guard against such future attempts to hoodwink or manipulate the administration or other agencies of government. Early on, the country was learning something of the president's style: he was a delegator, loyal to subordinates and prob-ably naive in his judgments of politicians, slow to anger and only rarely given to censure, and reluctant to dismiss subordinates under almost any circumstances.

8

Beyond Our Shores

Grant's handling of his administration's first domestic crisis was lag-gard and uncertain, though culminating finally in decisive action. In foreign policy, addressing several challenges early in the administra-tion, his leadership was more promising. Moreover, in his relation-ship with the ablest member of his cabinet, Secretary of State Hamilton Fish, he revealed a hitherto unexpected capacity for deliberation and consultation. It would serve the country well.

In foreign policy, nineteenth-century presidents operated in an ambience described in 1889 by Senator Henry Cabot Lodge: "Our relations with foreign nations today fill but a slight place in American politics and excite . . . a languid interest. We have separated ourselves so completely from the affairs of other people." The United States, declared Andrew Johnson's secretary of state, William Seward, a frus-trated expansionist, seeks no conquest. Its preoccupations are almost wholly internal—with certain exceptions having little to do with the conscious strategic aims any of foreign "policy." The Monroe Doctrine was an article of faith, and perceived challenges to it were bound to excite concern, of course; but the naval and military resources of the country would scarcely have permitted an aggressive overseas policy beyond the Western Hemisphere, even if the nation had favored it. The nation's preoccupations were domestic ones.

When Grant left Washington in the early summer of 1869 for an extended holiday on the New Jersey shore, he asserted "policy enough for the present," but separate challenges in foreign affairs presented themselves almost immediately. The first, and most serious, of these involved Great Britain, America's most important trading partner and the master of the world's seas, with whom the United States had long had rocky relations, especially during the Civil War. In June 1861, a Confederate agent, James D. Bulloch, was sent to England to contract with private shipbuilders for the construction of commerce raiders, warships for a new navy desperate for the means to challenge and destroy Union shipping. Although British law forbade the construction of naval ships to be used in wars in which Great Britain was not a belligerent, a labored interpretation of the law could be construed to permit the building of ships that might be "fitted out" elsewhere (i.e., what you do with the new ship after we make it seaworthy is your business). One such vessel, the *Florida*, had left Liverpool, later to be prepared in Bermuda for a career of commerce raiding; the second, its shipyard label "290," was obviously being prepared for belligerent purposes. The British foreign secretary ordered the ship seized. Bulloch, learning of the foreign secretary's intention, sent the vessel to sea on a "trial run." The ship proceeded directly to the Azores, there to be fitted out, far from British waters, as a commerce raider. She was given the name *Alabama*.

Alabama was enormously successful in its mission, destroying or capturing some sixty-four Union merchant ships in a two-year career, often replenishing in British colonial ports. It was finally sunk in battle in June 1864 with the USS *Kearsage*.

Toward the end of the Johnson administration, late in 1868, Britain and the United States agreed on a treaty for the settlement of American claims arising from the *Alabama* episode, a treaty which, however, seemed unduly favorable to the British in the eyes of many in Congress, and it was voted down in the Senate, 54–1, in April 1869. The chairman of the Senate Foreign Relations Committee, Charles Sumner of Massachusetts, delivered a bellicose speech against the treaty, claiming that the *Alabama*'s direct depredations were but a small part of England's real culpability during the war. As a matter of fact, he argued, such commerce raiders and Britain's encouraging attitude toward the South had served to prolong the Civil War *by two years!*

He hinted that a fair recompense would be the forfeiture of Canada. Not only had the aggregate cost of "the vaster commerce driven from the ocean"—which Sumner put at $110 million—been far greater than earlier estimates, the war's prolongation now implied a total British indebtedness of $2 billion, in his estimation.

Charles Sumner was among the most powerful men in the Senate, entirely used to having his way in foreign affairs. Though friendly to Grant's new secretary of state, Hamilton Fish, he resented Grant's failure to consult him when considering candidates, and he condescended to Fish once the New Yorker came into office. He was gratified at the appointment of the renowned historian and diplomat John Lothrop Motley as minister to England: Motley was a close friend and protégé, and Sumner believed that all future negotiations could, in effect, now be supervised by the ablest of American students and practitioners of foreign policy: himself.

For a man of Hamilton Fish's temperament, Sumner's bluster was less a threat to authority than an obstacle quietly to be surmounted or worked around. When the president learned through his former aide Adam Badeau, now the secretary of the American legation in London, that Sumner was communicating directly with Motley, presuming to instruct him as to the demands he should make on the British, Grant told Fish that he wanted the minister recalled and dismissed. But Fish persuaded Grant to leave him where he was and simply to marginalize him; in this way, they would not risk jeopardizing negotiations at this point, instead allowing Fish to look after the process. In addition, both Grant and Fish were now reluctant to take the British to task for their early recognition of Confederate belligerency because the president himself was being asked to consider extending belligerent status to Cuban rebels pressing for independence from Spain.

This insurgency in Cuba had flared before, but it had now attracted broad American public attention and popular support. What little the public understood of its causes was bound to excite its support—the Cuban rebels were fighting for their freedom from a distant, authoritarian regime. Grant, at Fish's urging, resisted the clamor to recognize the rebels, who had no government or army, even after Congress passed a resolution in April 1869 promising to support the president should he decide to intervene. Grant was also being pressured by his closest friend in the cabinet, John Rawlins, who had a financial interest in urging and was therefore promoting recognition for the rebels and, if necessary, American military intervention. Far more formidable in Grant's mind was the implicit threat of war with Spain, which maintained a large fleet off Cuba, and which sometimes stopped American shipping and arrested American civilians. At this point, providentially, word came through intermediaries that the ruling junta in Madrid would be willing to consider Cuban independence, in return for a cash payment. Grant and Fish agreed on a memorandum to be presented the Spaniards, one that provided for Cuban independence, payment of an indemnity by the Cubans, and the abolition of slavery. The new American consul in Madrid, former major general Daniel Sickles, was instructed to present the American terms.

Spain, however, proved unwilling to oblige such terms, and fighting now escalated on the island. In the cabinet Rawlins passionately pleaded for American intervention. The popular press took up the cry, the *New York Sun* even labeling the administration "deficient in character." But Grant and Fish maintained what had essentially become an attitude of watchful waiting, refusing to be forced into a recognition of rebel belligerency. They would commit the United States to efforts to mediate, but nothing more.

Grant restated his unwillingness to recognize belligerency in his annual message to Congress in December, and he successfully tamped down a possible joint resolution of Congress the following June, the resolution losing, 70 votes to 100, in the House. The intervention by the world's most famous soldier, an intervention on the side of peace, made a particularly powerful impact—not unlike Dwight Eisenhower's unwillingness to commit American ground forces to Indochina in 1954.

Orville Babcock, the White House secretary, had served on Grant's staff since the latter's appointment as general in chief in March 1864. He united several talents and expertises. He had graduated near the head of his class at West Point; he was a trained engineer; he worked rapidly and accurately in translating the president's needs and wishes into efficient action; he was likable and gregarious; and he was utterly loyal to Grant. The president selected him in June 1869 to perform a reconnaissance of the Caribbean nation of Santo Domingo, known today as the Dominican Republic. Babcock was given a letter of introduction to the president of the republic, Buenaventura Baez, and detailed instructions from Secretary of State Fish as to his duties. He had no diplomatic authority whatever. Rather he was to gather information for a report on Santo Domingo's resources—its minerals and agriculture; the nature of its government and administration; and, most important, its feelings toward the United States. The emissary was accompanied on the trip by Joseph Warren Fabens, an American living abroad, who three months earlier had astonished the new secretary of state by delivering a memorandum from the republic in which its president offered his country to the United States as a "free and independent state."

Although Fish instinctively disapproved, he had brought the matter before Grant and the cabinet. It was not the first time such an opportunity had presented itself, and the proposal was appealing due to the country's geopolitical attractiveness—it had both a strategic location and a superb natural harbor in Samana Bay. The bay could serve as a coaling station for naval ships and was an obvious port for vessels sailing to or from the Isthmus of Panama. Among the project's early enthusiasts was one of the president's oldest and dearest friends, Rear Admiral David Ammen, who had grown up with Grant in Georgetown and who had once saved the future president from drowning. He and Grant saw each other often in Washington; a place at the table was always laid for Ammen at lunch on Sunday in the White House.

Both Fabens and another American, William Cazneau, were friends of Baez; all stood to profit handsomely from any positive outcome—the lease of Samana Bay, a treaty, outright annexation. Fish and others were suspicious of all three, and of others that, they were hearing, had various financial stakes in the enterprise.

Babcock brought back his report. He also presented a draft memorandum in which President Baez offered Santo Domingo for
annexation or, alternatively, Samana Bay for two million dollars.
Meantime the American press had begun talking up the possibilities
of such an agreement, in editorials that called Santo Domingo "rich
beyond estimation in mines of gold, silver, and lead, [with] magnifi-
cent tropical forests [and] plains of amazing fertility." The public
was being titillated.

At the president's instruction, Fish prepared a draft treaty of
annexation, dated October 19, 1869. The cabinet was divided on
the project, but Babcock was sent back to Santo Domingo, where
he oversaw the signing of two instruments: one for annexation, the
other for Samana, should the first be turned down in Congress. In
all this activity, as the historian Allan Nevins observes, Grant
revealed an extraordinary naïveté as to procedure—about what in
another century would be called "process." In the same way that
Grant had recruited Hamilton Fish to be his secretary of state in an
astonishingly offhand manner, he no more moderated and led a
cabinet discussion of the venture than he had convened councils of
war when he was a general. It had simply seemed to him to be a
good thing to do; the wish was father not to the thought but to
action of the kind a general might order on a campaign. And once
committed to such an enterprise, Grant was as always temperamen-
tally indisposed to let go of it short of success—or definitive defeat.
Grant appears to have been attracted to the island republic (large
enough "to sustain the entire colored population of the United
States, should it choose to emigrate") as an acquisition that would
act in part as a force providing economic leverage for freedmen:
"What I desired above all," he said later, "was to secure a retreat for
that portion of the laboring classes of our former slave states, who
might find themselves under unbelievable pressure."

It finally occurred to the president that Charles Sumner should
be brought on board. Soon after Babcock's return he made an
evening call at Sumner's residence and argued his best case for
Sumner's support. An almost unimaginable cultural gulf separated
the two men, but Grant gamely made what he thought was a per-

suasive case for annexation, and he left with an understanding (so he thought) that Sumner would support the venture. He could not have been more wrong. Sumner was implacably opposed, and he soon carried most of the Foreign Affairs Committee with him, in recommending, 5–2, that the treaty be defeated. During the consequent debate, before the vote of the full Senate, Grant lobbied tirelessly for the treaty, with a view especially countering rumors of financial windfalls that interested parties might realize, and promising restrictions that would prevent such possibilities. The treaty was voted down in the Senate on June 30, 1870, nineteen Republicans joining ten Democrats to ensure its defeat.

(Grant's obsession, however, did not die easily. He got Congress to create, grudgingly, a commission to study Santo Domingo further, and its report to Congress in April 1871 made a careful and objective case in favor of annexation, giving Grant a satisfying though modest vindication. But by this time the Senate had moved on, and nothing came of it.)

The day after the Senate rejected the treaty, Grant told Fish to fire Motley as a public demonstration of Grant's unwillingness to tolerate Sumner's pretensions as an architect of American foreign policy. Much later Grant would insist that no motive of retribution prompted his action; he simply wanted, and needed, and ought to have, a leader of the same party in the Senate whose views on foreign relations were those that would promote useful collaboration between them. Behind the scenes, Fish and Grant both believed Sumner to be an obstructive crank, self-absorbed, self-righteous, mischievous. Sumner now became an implacable enemy.

Britain and the United States renewed their *Alabama* discussions in Washington in January 1871, through the useful and emollient counsel of the Canadian diplomat John Rose. Within four weeks Fish and the British minister, Edward Thorton, were able to persuade their respective governments to appoint commissions of five representatives each, not only to resolve the *Alabama* dispute but to address and if possible settle all outstanding issues between the United States and Britain, including those of fisheries and fishing rights and the ownership of the San Juan Islands in Puget Sound.

The work of the joint commission began in Washington in February and was completed in May with the signing of the Washington Treaty. The agreement provided that England would acknowledge culpability in the *Alabama* depredations, referring to an international tribunal in Geneva the question of indirect and direct claims for damages done to American shipping. At a special session of the Senate later in May, the treaty was overwhelmingly ratified, 50–12, and a formal ceremony in London on June 17, 1871, completed the long labor. The president announced the treaty's effective date as July 4. The Geneva arbitration commission, ignoring the issue of indirect claims, ordered the British to pay the United States an indemnity of $15.5 million.

The Washington Treaty is regarded as a landmark in the history of western diplomacy, and as a resolution of the last serious threat to what was becoming a special relationship between the world's oldest surviving democratic powers. In Hamilton Fish American diplomacy had found a worthy descendant of John Quincy Adams, just as he would prove to be the lineal ancestor of later American secretaries of state who tended to support close cooperation with Britain. As for Grant, he revealed a style of leadership—in all but military matters—that rested on a foundation of cultivated instinct, not expertise: on his ability to identify and sustain in office men of requisite ability and character. He was sensitive to the strictures, as he understood them, of the Monroe Doctrine and to insults to the flag abroad. He had no comprehensive foreign policy, and he was fortunate to serve when challenges to American interests abroad were slight. His collaboration in the Washington Treaty effort entitles him, however, to respect as a president who quietly superintended the nation's foreign policy at a quiet time. And like most soldier-presidents, he proved to be a closet moderate.

9

Reconstruction

Reconstruction denotes an unhappy time in American history. It is a label loosely applied to the decade after Appomattox, whose principal political preoccupation was the full reintegration of the states of the former Confederacy into the Union, and, prerequisite and concomitant both, the attainment of full unfettered American citizenship, its privileges and its duties, by black Americans. In the common consciousness it subsists today mainly as the second part of high school and college courses once standard: "Civil War and Reconstruction." Its way was supremely difficult and tortuous. Abraham Lincoln in his first inaugural address in 1861 had appealed to the better angels of Americans' natures, but after four years of Civil War, followed by military occupation in the South, congressional Reconstruction, the presidency of Andrew Johnson, the founding and accelerated growth of the Ku Klux Klan and hundreds of regional and local terrorist groups, this appeal was but a forlorn echo by the time Grant took office eight years later. The South hated military Reconstruction. If it accepted the Thirteenth Amendment, which ended chattel slavery, its acceptance of the Fourteenth and Fifteenth Amendments, which effectually made black Americans citizens and gave them the right to vote, was sullen and begrudging at best. Much of the South remained irreconcilable; it despised black Americans and considered them unfit for the usages of citizenship. The culture of the day is littered with commentaries on Negro unsuitability for such responsibilities—in both North and South.

Effectual Reconstruction faced a gross retinue of obstacles: northern frustration, weariness, and apathy, not to mention a populace that had come to resent the seemingly unending demands of Reconstruction—especially the redirection of money and energy to its needs—and which greeted each new law or achievement as an explicit cause for ending the government's role in the business. There was also the Republican recognition that, depending on how the party responded to what it understood as each new demand of the process, its fortunes—remaining in power or being turned out—would be directly implicated. Indeed, the Republican party itself remained divided on how best to proceed. A rising generation of party leaders, men in middle age, many of whom had not served in the war, were far more interested in process, patronage, and power than in actively servicing the moral imperatives of their postwar obligations to freedmen.

The challenges thus facing the Grant administration, bewilderingly multiform and, taken together, almost insoluble, present an extraordinary parallel to another melancholy episode in American history: the war in Vietnam. In each case those who labored to make a successful policy tended to impute to their adversaries the reactions and responses they themselves would be likely to feel or to make. In each case hopes, frail and weary, came to trump cold-eyed judgment. "You have not yet begun to consider what sort of men are these Athenians whom you may have to fight," the Corinthians warned Spartan leaders in the latter's assembly. You cannot imagine, that is to say, how different they are from yourselves. Things you revere, they abominate; actions you may take to demonstrate goodwill and magnanimity, they will see as demonstrations of weakness of the most abject kind. Your notion of how prolonged war, desperate and savage, has affected our psyches demonstrates an utter lack of understanding of our culture, our values, the cherished elements of our heritage—ours in the South, ours in Hanoi. You do not understand us; you presume to impose your will upon us, but you will fail. For there is a final consideration in the analogy: we are patient, and you are not. The patient assurance of southern Democrats, "redeemers" of the South, and the North Vietnamese leadership's sustaining certitude that America would soon tire of its costly commitment in Southeast Asia, was richly vindicated. Washington's ability to sustain an unpopular and costly policy was threatened, weakened, and finally overcome by the steady and implacable patience of its adversary.

Reconstruction during the Grant presidency is generally characterized as irresolute, as vacillating between extremes of conciliation and reprisal, with military intervention often determined not by the requirements of the local situation (Ku Klux Klan terrorism used to keep blacks from voting in South Carolina), but by calculations of partisan politics (deciding whether to send the army into Mississippi based on its likely effect on Republican chances in the Ohio gubernatorial elections). In Vietnam the idea that a determined enemy could be brought to book by inflicting upon him the kind of punishment that Americans might imagine would do the trick with Americans was the most egregious mistake of the war. In each case, American leaders—Reconstructionists of the 1860s and '70s, Pentagon officials of the 1960s and '70s—believed that their adversaries would react in the ways needed to serve Washington's policy.

It is often a liability of democracy that its citizens cannot for a long time sustain support for policies and actions that, however noble their goals, do not demonstrate measurable progress. Moral stamina, as historians call it, is a perishable commodity in the American polity. Abraham Lincoln might urge that the nation take increased devotion to the cause for which the Union dead had given the last full measure of devotion, but citizens of neither 1863 nor 1875 could agree among themselves as to the real nature of that cause, and what labors were necessary, and right, to secure its final achievement. As the years wore on and the war edged further into the past, many northern citizens had had enough and were ready to move on. For them, this was the meaning of Grant's famous injunction *"Let us have peace."*

The enunciation of the signature plea *Let us have peace* was an early element in the establishment of what would immediately become a pattern. An achievement, an event, a declaration is made: some success of Reconstruction. The response, at first tentative, then invariable, is a relieved acknowledgment that this particular achievement, event, or declaration marks the real end of a necessary involvement in the war's tangled, dispiriting aftermath in the South, the last prerequisite to the completion of our obligation. Grant is elected, now we are relieved of our burden; he is a man who can fix things. The Fifteenth Amendment has passed Congress. Once ratified, it will guarantee the vote to the black man—he will then be arbiter and captain of his own future. We can wash our hands of the business. The Enforcement Acts will ensure swift punishment for anyone who attempts to violate the rights of black Americans or institute terror in the South. That should complete our duty.

Grant had been bequeathed a set of political challenges together more severe than those that have greeted all American presidents save only two (Lincoln and Franklin Roosevelt) at their inaugurations. But by far the largest and most difficult was the huge welter of unresolved issues subsumed under the term *Reconstruction*. Historians have long undervalued or ignored this element of the Grant presidency, drawn as they have been to the "scandals" of the administration, to issues of foreign and economic policy, and so on. At the turn of the twentieth century and down to midcentury, Johnson and Grant and the congressional leaders who oversaw Reconstruction have been treated as misguided zealots who profoundly undervalued the counsels of "thinking men." Carpetbaggers were seen as bloodsucking opportunists battening upon a helpless and impoverished southern economy. Southern Democrats were reactionaries, mostly bigots, and a large lunatic fringe among them was determined to destroy the privileges given black citizens—often in massacres whose names still disgrace the annals of southern history.

Each generation writes its own histories. Ours is beginning to see Reconstruction as Dryden said Chaucer saw life: steadily and whole. Compared to what followed, with the inauguration of Grant's successor, Rutherford B. Hayes, in March 1877, which was but an exhausted and timid acquiescence in Things As They Are in the South, the Grant administration's efforts seem honorably (if not always intelligently) framed to preserve the war's best legacy. Grant saw his charge as to enforce the obligations of the Fourteenth and Fifteenth Amendments and to reconcile what were probably irreconcilable duties: to protect the freedmen, to conciliate the South, to sustain the Republican party, and, after 1873, to address the needs of a country reeling from economic depression.

In a technical sense it can be said that Reconstruction ended in February 1871, when the last of the ten southern states that had undergone "military Reconstruction" saw their congressional delegations reseated in the House and Senate. Four states composed this group—Virginia, Mississippi, Texas, and Georgia—and Grant, only a month after his inauguration, had sent Congress a letter asking that it move swiftly to approve the process by which these states could be represented in Congress again. Certain requirements had been established for them, including the approval of a "disfranchising clause" that denied all political appointments and government positions to a large category of former Confederate soldiers and officials. Some 150,000 men were affected. Grant believed it reasonable to allow the states to vote separately on the different clauses, even knowing that the states would likely vote against disfranchisement. All did. But Congress, satisfied with their approval of the other clauses, voted to seat their representatives. The state of Georgia was treated separately, because its legislators had excluded blacks from the state assembly, but it too was finally certified as having complied late in 1870, and its representatives were admitted to Congress in February 1871.

A general amnesty for all who swore an oath before the war to defend the Constitution was not signed into law until May 1872. It left only five hundred former Confederate officers without pardon, removing the disability from holding office for the great majority of those so punished.

The U.S. Army remained the only federal agency capable of enforcing southern compliance with federal law. Grant, himself constrained by the Constitution from using it in this way, except in rare circumstances, was by conviction reluctant to employ the army as a military police force. And so in the spring of 1870 Congress established a federal Department of Justice, with the attorney general, already a cabinet officer and presidential adviser, now the head of a functioning department whose mission was to ensure compliance with the law. To assist the attorney general, Congress also authorized a new office, that of solicitor general, the government's chief attorney. In succession to Ebenezer Rockwood Hoar, whom Grant had dismissed to gain southern support for the Santo Domingo venture in exchange for a southern cabinet member, the president appointed Amos T. Ackerman, a northerner by birth who had lived in Georgia since boyhood. Ackerman was a man of incorruptible integrity, completely devoted to the aims of Reconstruction. As the first solicitor general, he selected General Benjamin H. Bristow, the U.S. attorney for Kentucky, who had compiled an admirable civil rights record in that state. Ackerman's and Bristow's overriding mission immediately became one of curbing antiblack violence and intimidation in the South, because it was becoming clear that the expressions of relief in the North at the news of the ratification of the Fifteenth Amendment had been unwarranted. Grant's former quartermaster general, Montgomery Meigs, warned sharply of the South's "active guilt . . . they cannot enslave but they will outrage and oppress. Their hearts are not changed."

In the message he sent Congress, accompanying the secretary of state's promulgation of the ratified Fifteenth Amendment, Grant communicated the passion of his own conviction. This amendment, he said, "is . . . a measure of grander importance than any other one act of the kind from the foundation of our free government to the present day." He continued:

> I call the attention therefore of the newly enfranchised race to the importance of their striving in every honorable manner to make themselves worthy of their new privileges. To the race more favored heretofore by our laws I would say withhold no legal privileges of advancement to the new citizen.

The message rehearses the familiar Jeffersonian exhortation that all citizens educate themselves on the issues that touch the common weal, in preparation for the duties of voting.

In December 1866 Frederick Douglass, a loyal and devoted admirer of Grant's, had urged the importance of giving "every loyal citizen the elective franchise—a right and power which will be ever present, and will form a wall of fire for his protection." But the only walls of fire being formed in the early 1870s in the South were literal walls, and the incendiaries were mainly members of the Ku Klux Klan, determined to preserve white supremacy, destroy the Republican party in the South, and ensure the restoration of all prewar usages, social and political. In rage, numbers, and resources, the Klan grew to its maximum strength during the first Grant administration. It struck throughout the South, doing its work mainly at night, its instruments comprising kidnapping, murder, arson, beatings, and the terror induced by not knowing when, or where, it would strike next (black churches were particularly favored targets), together with the certain knowledge that local law enforcement, when not actually conniving in such activities, would itself be sufficiently intimidated to do nothing.

Evidences of voter intimidation and fraud, both in the midterm elections in 1870 and in local elections throughout the South, and through poorly organized efforts to overthrow the Republican governments of Florida and South Carolina, as well as a congressional investigation of Klan violence and intimidation, prompted Grant's hand. Specifically, the Republican governor of South Carolina implored Grant to send federal troops to deal with terrorists—and Grant obliged him. He also asked the Speaker of the House in March 1871 to consider framing a bill that would specifically facilitate northern efforts to quash widespread terrorism against blacks in the South. Grant went to Congress personally to lobby for the legislation, arguing that the states did not have the resources to deal successfully with the challenge and that it was the federal government's responsibility to protect citizens and voters in the exercise of their rights as citizens.

The Ku Klux Klan bill passed Congress April 20, and Grant issued a proclamation drawing southerners' attention to the act, urging compliance and promising swift and sure federal action if violence and intimidation continued. Two weeks after the act became law, Grant sent troops into various southern locations, including a large contingent into South Carolina, and during the remainder of the year, federal grand juries indicted some three thousand Klansmen and others for acts of violence, and many were convicted. The elections the following year were called by one scholar "the fairest and most democratic presidential election in the South until 1968."

Critics of Grant often describe him as a hands-off executive, lacking the zealous temperament needed to promote reform over the forces of stasis and avarice. But there is another kind of zeal, and it was this kind that distinguished Grant's commitment to uphold what he understood to be the legacy of victory in the Civil War: not the aggressive zeal of the reformer who stakes out new positions on contentious issues, but an implacable commitment to a principle already established. Such commitments permit and even suggest tactical compromise, but the depth of Grant's commitment to Reconstruction seemed to grow stronger as resistance to the realization of what he believed itself became more determined. The identification of the Democratic party with positions that seemed aimed on destroying the hard-won gains of black Americans seemed to the president a betrayal of all they had gained by the war and a betrayal of those who had labored to make its results permanent. Grant said, "I am a Republican because I am an American, and because I believe the first duty of an American—the paramount duty— is to save the results of the war, and save our credit."

The Greek poet Archilochus, known to us from a few surviving fragments of preclassical poetry, made a familiar distinction between hedgehogs and foxes: "The fox knows many things, but the hedgehog knows one big thing." By political conviction, which for Ulysses Grant was coterminous with moral conviction, the president was a hedgehog: he believed in the preservation of what he understood to be the legacy of the terrible war that he had fought under the leadership of Abraham Lincoln. He had come by that conviction in a hard school. The war in which he had begun his service as a civilian volunteer in the governor's office was to have been a simple affair of military chastisement: the Union would defeat, quickly and without great effusion of blood, a misguided enemy—errant, erring sisters, states that had followed a false god that seduced them to fight for their independence from the Union. Within a year he had seen that the war would be no such thing, and by 1863 he understood that slavery was the issue central to the war's resolution, and that victory meant the end of slavery, along with the citizenship and enfranchisement of blacks. To achieve that end guaranteed bitter contention of the kind that might survive the achievement of the end itself. It required constitutional amendments with strong enforcement mechanisms. Enforcement became therefore the duty of the national government, whatever interventionist scruples might impede the willingness to execute that duty. The southern states, most of them "redeemed" by 1871, simply would not enforce the law, and yet Grant's own party had also begun to abandon its obligation, its congressional leaders no longer the passionate foot soldiers of the Northern Cause. The president— and here lies his title to the gratitude of succeeding generations— was its best and steadiest guarantor.

In war Ulysses Grant was not especially distinguished as a tactician; as a strategist and leader, he stood far above his contemporaries. As steadfast upholder of the war's final legacy during his term as president, Grant was the central force in the achievement of civil rights for blacks, the most stalwart and reliable among all American presidents for the next eighty years.

Historians have criticized Grant for the partisan bias in his decisions to authorize military intervention in the southern states, but it was his most effective response to southern Democrats and sympathetic terrorist organizations whose main purpose was to "keep down" African-Americans and the Republican candidates and officeholders who represented their best hopes. The "bias" reflects credit on Grant. Frederick Douglass offered this encomium:

> To Grant more than any other man the Negro owes his enfranchisement and the Indian a humane policy. In the matter of the protection of the freedman from violence his moral

courage surpassed that of his party: his place at its head was given to timid men, and the country was allowed to drift, instead of stemming the current.

Grant himself was at pains to assert the lamentable association of party, in his time, with race.

> Under existing conditions the Negro votes the Republican ticket because he knows his friends are of that party. Many a good citizen votes the opposite . . . because, generally, he is opposed to Negro rule. This is a most delusive cry. Treat the Negro as a citizen and a voter, as he is and must remain, and soon parties will be divided not on the color line, but on principle.

Grant later confided rather ruefully to his traveling companion and *New York Herald* reporter John Russell Young that he "did not see what the North can do that has not been done, unless we surrender the results of the war." As Grant's first term in office drew to a close and he prepared for the reelection campaign of 1872, he sensed that the northern wing of the party was drawing steadily away from his own commitment to the freedmen. And yet he remained their champion, despite the waning support of such a position.

The president willing to shoulder what had become an unacceptable burden for virtually everyone else in government was the same man who had protested being separated from his infantry company in Mexico to be assigned to a safe staff position, the same citizen who had put his career on the line to ensure that the government make good on his promise to Lee at Appomattox: a man prepared to do what he believed was the right thing to do.

10

The Original Inhabitants

Ulysses Grant, one of the most talented writers to occupy the White House, labored in writing his inaugural addresses and annual messages to Congress not to disappoint the expectations of his audiences. He imagined that such lofty occasions require a certain kind of language. It is extraordinary, the difference in tone and syntax between these set pieces, on the one hand, and the headlong clarity of his military orders and correspondence, not to mention the limber prose of his *Memoirs*. The first inaugural in places seems to labor to engage an audience that Grant senses is skeptical of the Fifteenth Amendment, extending the right to vote to blacks: "The question of suffrage is one which is likely to agitate the public. . . . It seems to me very desirable that the question should be settled now, and I entertain the hope . . ." et cetera.

Against such verbiage a paragraph toward the end of the address stands out starkly as a muscular statement of intent: "The proper treatment of *the original inhabitants of this land*, the Indian . . . I will favor any course which tends to their civilization and ultimate citizenship." The intent was clear and bold: Grant was asking for the endorsement of a policy aimed at making the Indians just like us, just like the white Americans who constituted almost all Grant's audience. For its time, Grant's statement of intent and the means he would select to make good his avowal were as unusual as they were bold. To use a word few historians have applied to Ulysses Grant the president, for anything, it was *noble*.

Grant's Philadelphia friend George W. Childs wrote that the president's service in the Pacific Northwest in the 1850s had led him to make "up his mind that if he ever had any influence or power it should be exercised to try to ameliorate the Indians' condition." It was pity, not passion, that first moved him. In letters to Julia he had noted that the Indians he saw were far too "insignificant in prowess and numbers to need much care or attention . . . and that this poor remainder . . . is fast wasting away before those blessings of 'civilization,' whisky and small pox." To Julia, who worried about his safety and who surely conceived of Indians as savages bent on killing soldiers, he wrote that "they were the most harmless people you ever saw . . . the whole race would be harmless and peaceable if they were not put upon by whites."

American settlers' treatment of the Indians was disgraceful. It was rationalized as a continuing expression of manifest destiny, as civilization overspreading an empty continent, as an enterprise to which its needs and talents and superior strength entitled it. Its tribunes justified massacres of Indians as the unfortunate but necessary retribution the natives had coming to them; in such slaughters as those of Sand Creek in eastern Colorado in 1864 and the Washita in Oklahoma in 1868, they provided the Indians with ample reason to mistrust any subsequent peace policy the government might proclaim. (To that time some 370 separate treaties had been made between Indians and government agencies, virtually all of them broken, and usually by white citizens.) The episode on the Washita, led by a young colonel named George Armstrong Custer, had in fact occurred only a year after the establishment of a peace commission under President Johnson, its mission to study the Indian question on the ground and to make recommendations for a permanent understanding between government and tribes. The Johnson panel included General Sherman, who was to write, only a year later, in a directive to General Sheridan, "I want you to go ahead, kill and punish the hostiles, capture and destroy the ponies . . . of the Cheyennes, Arapahoes, and

Kiowas. The more we kill this year, the less we would have to kill next year." The commission recommended that Congress appropriate money enough to move all the Plains Indians onto reservations, where these nomadic peoples would be taught to be farmers and artisans. The government would guarantee such necessities as those needed to ensure a strong start in their new lives.

But the monies were not appropriated, and the Indians soon began raiding in their traditional hunting grounds. A number of settlers were killed. It was against this background that Grant made his promise in his first inaugural. He had already met with a group of philanthropists led by the Philadelphian William Welsh, who convinced the president-elect that he needed to secure the promised congressional appropriation, but that now it was to be used to underwrite a new policy, one that would follow from a fresh examination of the issue by another commission, this one comprising private citizens.

The new departure and the work it undertook became known colloquially as the Quaker policy, as several of the first agents appointed were Friends. Other Protestant denominations were also represented among the appointed agents, the presumption being that such men would be incorruptible and of an evangelizing bent. It is a colossal irony: most whites who had ruined the Indians had claimed to do so in the name of promoting Christian culture; now a group of Christian missionaries would oversee their redemption and the domestication of their children. Barely less ironic to the public mind was the fact that the Union's foremost fighting general was the ardent steward of the new policy, if not its original author. The new "policy" envisaged the domestication of the Indians, through settlements on reservations: as farmers, artisans, educable workers who would themselves serve local Indian communities. Schools would be available to all Indian children; the Christian gospel would be preached. The Indian was to be treated with solicitude and fairness.

Working through his secretary of the interior, David Cox, and Ely Parker, himself a full-blooded Seneca, Grant oversaw a radical change in the treatment of American Indians. Successive annual messages left no doubt as to the sincerity of his commitment: "Wars of extermination are demoralizing and wicked. Our superiority should make us lenient toward the Indian. . . . A system which looks to the extinction of a race is too horrible for a nation to adopt without entailing upon itself the wrath of all Christendom."

The Board of Commissioners reported scathingly on the activities of the Indian agents, men who had been appointed through political patronage, their positions notorious for graft and fraud, in which many had realized annual profits many times their salaries of fifteen hundred dollars. The commissioners not only recommended new appointees but also argued for a new policy, in Congress and in the press. Moreover, Grant appointed army officers to some vacancies—a move that congressional critics opposed, for it removed patronage opportunities from their oversight and control. Grant's response to this was to fill further vacant Indian agent positions with religious appointees. He continued, also, to insist on annual congressional appropriations necessary to sustain the work, usually in the face of strong opposition.

Grant's peace policy was generally celebrated in the eastern press but deplored in the West and in Congress. The president's two most important military subordinates, Sherman and Sheridan, loyal and devoted to their chief, nonetheless thought the policy misjudged. One imagines their thinking: What's gotten into Grant? On the Great Plains a policy of fairness and conciliation seemed the work of an obtuse administration that simply didn't understand the nature of the Indian character as most whites there saw it—violent, shiftless, brutish, and filled with hatred for whites. Magnanimity and conciliation did not work in the reconstruction of the South; how could they be expected to prevail in the West? A consequence of such attitudes was invariable: when there was trouble, when Indian tribes were reported to have conducted raids or murdered settlers, the army's response was disproportionate and hamfisted. More than 170 Indians were annihilated on the Marias River in Montana in January 1870—mostly families of warriors, many already suffering from smallpox—in a punitive expedition for a raid by a Piegan war party. In another incident, in January 1873, the department commander in the Northwest, General Edward Canby, was murdered at a meeting with the Modoc Indians in northern

California. (The meeting had been called to settle a military stale-mate between the Modocs and army forces sent to shepherd them onto reservations.) Canby was unarmed, as was the local Indian agent, also murdered. "You will be fully justified in their extermination" was Sherman's response.

But by far the greatest challenge to Grant's new policy followed in the wake of the discovery of gold in the Black Hills in the Dakota Territory. The discovery was made in the heart of a huge reservation guaranteed the Sioux in 1868 by the Treaty of Fort Laramie. The historian Jean Edward Smith notes Sheridan's recollection that Grant had acceded to Sheridan's view that the army was powerless and undermanned to protect the reservation from the flood of white gold diggers now flooding the area. Sheridan was ordered to force the Indians onto a part of the reservation and to keep an eye on them. It was this directive, however Sheridan understood it, that led to an army initiative to surround the Indians: three large forces would converge on them from the east, south, and west. Custer's Seventh Cavalry, marching from Fort Abraham Lincoln on the Missouri River, isolated from the other two columns, and led by a commander who loved to fight and who lacked useful intelligence as to his enemy's strength and whereabouts, was wiped out at the Little Bighorn on June 25, 1876.

The effect of the massacre—"The Last Stand"—was to gut the peace policy, to make disillusioned cynics of many of its remaining supporters, and to excite easterners' thirst for vengeance. It also mocked the self-congratulatory atmosphere of the Philadelphia Centennial Exposition, then under way. Sheridan now set about his work with a serious vengeance, and within four years the Plains were quiet.

Grant fought for and supported during his administration an Indian policy that for its time was humane, generous in instinct and intent, far ahead of the conventional cultural and political wisdom of its day. It failed to understand that what needed to be protected was Indian culture itself. But the attempt was admirably conceived. It is a testimony to the odd blindness of American historiography that it has never received its due.

11

Reform, Rebuff, Reelection

Hopeful citizens had credited the new president with an unusual array of traits of character. Among them were the effacement, or rather submersion, of self in mighty missions: service without calculation of reward or risk. Oliver Wendell Holmes believed he had seen it in Grant during the Civil War: "I cannot get over the impression he made on me . . . that of an entire loss of selfhood in a great aim, which made all the common influences which stir up other people as nothing to him." Allied to this was Grant's ability to judge whether others possessed the same quality; and his determination to employ such people in the important work of governance. Merit, tested and proved, would surely be the only criterion of advancement to places of responsibility. Grant might be expected, in other words, to find and hire the best men; political considerations of the crasser sort would no longer drive appointments. He had not sought offices or promotions for himself; he would not tolerate self-seeking in others. Indeed, between election and inauguration he was rumored to have ordered all applications for positions in the administration thrown into the wastebasket.

By the end of the Civil War more than fifty thousand citizens were employed in the (civilian) federal bureaucracy, the largest numbers in the Departments of the Treasury and Post Office. There were sizable contingents, also, in the Departments of the Interior, Navy, and War. Criteria for appointment and promotion were usually unstated, but competence and training beyond minimums were not usually prerequisites for continuing tenure. Rather, federal appointments were used to reward political supporters and contributors small and large. Further, almost all civil service employees were regularly assessed contributions for the campaigns of the parties that had appointed them. By the mid-1840s, just as Grant was leaving West Point, the incoming Democratic administration of James K. Polk thought nothing of replacing more than 13,500 of 16,000 postmasters who had been appointed by the Whig presidents William Henry Harrison and his successor, John Tyler.

By such means, the national parties sustained themselves in office. Presidents, senators, congressmen made full use of patronage resources. Turnover was very high, promotion errant and almost always without examination. The idea that objective judgments as to qualifications should be demanded would have struck party leaders as unworkable at best, if not preposterous. President Lincoln had ignored what had at least been identified as a serious problem. His preoccupations were with issues far larger than this. And few American presidents have ever made appointments to senior ranks of the army on grounds more flagrantly "political" than Lincoln did, as Ulysses Grant had to learn and relearn during his tenure as commander in the West and as general in chief. Andrew Johnson, in circumstances somewhat different, continued Lincoln's practice; it was his determination to rid himself of an incompliant secretary of war, Stanton, that led directly to his final downfall and the impeachment he barely survived.

This spoils system particularly excited the indignation of what today might be called public intellectuals—editors, professors, journalists, pundits—most of them from New York and New England. An early champion of reform was the Rhode Islander Thomas Allen Jenckes, a member of Congress since 1862 and the first to introduce a comprehensive bill for the reform of the civil service—legislation that stipulated open competitive examinations for appointment and for promotion. A board of civil service commissioners would oversee the new program; it would develop rules and regulations; its members themselves would be guaranteed a five-year tenure and immunity from dismissal. Clearly the administration of Andrew Johnson had had a quickening effect on Jenckes's determination to secure legislation, but his bill failed to pass. The issue remained, now taken up by men like Charles Eliot Norton, man of letters, coeditor of the *North American Review,* and a founder of the *Nation;* E. L. Godkin, editor of the *Nation;* and George William Curtis, an editor at *Harper's.* In his delighted anticipation of a Grant regime, in which he believed the new president would take a strong lead from the start in seeking out and appointing "the best men," Norton typified the responses of his circle: "Grant grows daily in my respect and confidence. . . . [He] is so simple, so sensible, so strong and so magnanimous." But Norton also suggested to his friend Curtis that the latter mention to the administration that he, Norton, would be an appropriate appointee to a European mission—as minister.

President Grant failed to gratify these inflated expectations; he saw patronage as Lincoln had seen it—as a political necessity whose influences need not be malign, provided honest partisans were recruited and appointed. "Honest partisanship is honest citizenship," one of Grant's successors would assert. Grant himself was bombarded by patronage requests, not excluding several from his own family and their friends. He made his father postmaster in Covington, Kentucky. He also discovered that the most principled and high-minded were no less importunate than the merely ambitious when it came to advancing their own claims or those of their friends. They were particularly drawn to the diplomatic service as a suitable venue for the exercise of their talents, as Charles Eliot Norton had suggested for himself. Grant understood also that requiring objective assessments of talent and fitness for civil service jobs could frighten or outrage his own allies in Congress, in the Senate particularly. Nonetheless he had seen the depredations of Andrew Johnson's abuse of the system, and so he was moved to act.

In his second annual message to Congress, in December 1870, he wrote:

> Always favoring practical reforms, I respectfully call your
> attention to one abuse of long standing which I would like to

see remedied by this Congress. It is a reform to the civil
service of this country. . . . I would have it govern, not the
tenure, but the manner of making all appointments. . . . The
present system does not secure the best men, and often not
even fit men, for public place.

Two members of the president's cabinet had already made a
start: Jacob D. Cox, at the Department of the Interior, and George
S. Boutwell, at the Treasury, both insisted on competitive exams for
certain positions and a careful vetting of qualifications in new
appointments. Congress remained reluctant to act—and the most
reluctant were the supporters of the president himself. Grant's old
friend John Logan thought of such reform as fundamentally anti-
democratic. It would lead to the advancement of idealists and intellectuals rather than practical men of affairs, men who would reliably
support the president in his work and the Republican party in
office. Reformers were nothing but "man-milliners," according to
Grant's senatorial champion Roscoe Conkling; yet another senator
called them "effeminate . . . unable to beget or to bear; possessing
neither fecundity nor virility; endowed with the contempt of men
and the derision of women, and doomed to sterility."

Without enthusiasm Congress nonetheless approved an 1871
bill to create a civil service commission that would be charged with
the overhaul of the system. The bill barely passed and just survived
a subsequent motion that would have voided it. The commission,
under George Curtis, recommended that examinations be required
for all civil service positions (with a few, senior, exceptions), that
each department have its own examining board, and "that no political assessments be allowed." Grant determined to implement these
recommendations at once but needed congressional approval for
them to become permanent. In a letter to a commission member he
concluded with a statement of settled conviction: "The choice of
Federal officers has come to be limited to those seeking office. A
true reform will let the office seek the man."

But Congress would not approve legislation that would make
reforms permanent, nor (three years later) would it even appropriate

twenty-five thousand dollars to keep the commission afloat. Despite repeated urgings from Grant, there would be no substantial reform of the civil service until the Pendleton Act of 1883.

Disappointed civil service reformers in the Northeast soon were attracted to a new movement, its earliest roots in Missouri, that would mature into a full-blown schism in the Republican party. The movement was a strange and ill-assorted coalescence of men with various grievances against the president and his principal congressional supporters. The Missourians had been provoked initially by a fervent desire to remove the penalties in the state constitution against those who had supported the South; and this grew into a later demand that the federal government remove itself from the affairs of the states entirely and that full amnesty be granted, along with the end of "bayonet rule," by which the army was enforcing federal regulations on several states. The Missourians found common cause with the liberal reformers, who were disappointed in the Grant administration, who called for dismantling the spoils system and the corruptions.

A national convention was called for May 1, 1872, in Cincinnati, at which the two groups sought common ground but found great differences of opinion instead. On the protective tariff, for example, the articulate eastern contingent argued that any change would endanger business: to lower the tariff would doom financial interests in the great banking houses of the East. But this position was directly the contrary of westerners'. And while all 4,500 delegates might agree that the federal government should withdraw altogether from the South, that it should maintain the Union, and that it should resist any reopening of the "questions settled by the Thirteenth, Fourteenth, and Fifteenth Amendments," their disagreement on the tariff was embarrassingly finessed in a platform avowal that the liberal Republicans—as they now called themselves—"remit the discussion of the subject to the people in their congressional districts, and the decision of the Congress thereon, wholly free from Executive interference."

Passion and venom were the portion of the convention's castigation of the president. An inattentive reader might have imagined himself listening to a denunciation of King George III: the convention's "Address to the People of the United States" asserted that Grant had "openly used the powers and opportunities of his high office for personal ends. He has kept notoriously corrupt and unworthy men in places of power and responsibilities. . . . He has interfered with tyrannical arrogance in the public affairs of States." Grant was depicted as lazy, with no thoughts other than of horses and cigars, the victim of a constitutional torpor that was deemed fatal in a chief executive.

The convention nominated Horace Greeley as its candidate, a selection that astounded many of the delegates and almost all those outside the convention who were counted on as prospective supporters of the movement. Greeley, the most famous and brilliant journalist of the nineteenth century, founder and editor of the *New York Tribune*, had argued with characteristic brio in behalf of both sides of most major issues for the Civil War and its aftermath. He was known as a strong supporter of high tariffs; he was on record, many times, as having been violently critical of the Democratic party, with whom the liberal Republicans proposed to ally themselves for the election. He seemed, further, to lack gravitas. In appearance he was a character out of illustrations in Dickens's novels: plump, with a bald red head like a pumpkin, frequently dressed in bizarre dusters, given to strange fads and nostrums—like arguing for the particular agricultural efficacy of human manure.

Nonetheless, the Democrats, lacking a strong national candidate of their own, were persuaded to adopt him as their standard-bearer at their convention later that summer, in Baltimore.

The issue of Grant's reelection was never in doubt, though the vigor of the liberal Republican effort at first caused a mild anxiety among Republicans, one of whom, Grant's Philadelphia friend George W. Childs, urged the president to campaign seriously. After flawlessly predicting the results of the coming election, using a pencil and a map, Grant told Childs that the only presidential campaigners who had been accomplished speakers (Stephen A. Douglas and Horatio Seymour) had both lost. "I am no public speaker and don't want to be beaten."

In the end, Grant did win handily, taking 56 percent of the

popular vote. He carried every northern state and several states of the old Confederacy. He had appealed, despite his inarticulateness and unwillingness to campaign, both to the "better angels" (to paraphrase Lincoln) of the voters' nature, in recommitting Republicans to sustaining the achievements of the war, and to the continuing gratitude and confidence of the huge numbers of veterans, their friends and relatives, who revered him as the military savior of the Union. The results of the election of 1872 demonstrate the liberal Republicans' continuing underestimation of Ulysses Grant's hold on the sentiment of the larger American public. In reelecting him, the people were voting for someone with whom they were comfortable, for someone they liked. His hold on their affections was not dissimilar to that of Ronald Reagan, however baffling that bond between ordinary citizen and president might have seemed to his opponents. Finally, in reelecting Ulysses Grant, they were (consciously or not) sustaining in office the man who had won the Civil War, and who was—they saw this plainly—the best guarantor of the preservation of its achievements.

12

Scandals

The familiar historical fallacy *post hoc, ergo propter hoc* holds that an event that happens afterward must have been caused by what went before. There is a related fallacy, for which there is no familiar Latin aphorism. This argues that simultaneity implies common causation. Because things—actions, events, attitudes—exist at the same time, their existence must be traced to common cause. Here is a familiar example: the political scandals and corruption of the 1870s, of the time Mark Twain was first to call the Gilded Age, would seem to have a common origin, if not cause: the Grant administration or, somehow, Grant himself. Richard Hofstadter wrote in 1948, simply, "Grant's administrations are notorious for their corruption." No elaboration necessary. This judgment seems positively benign when compared with another, much earlier in the century, that the Grant administration was "the nadir of national disgrace."

Toward the end of his second inaugural address the president wrote, with a sullen passion that must have shocked those who heard him read it:

> I did not ask for place or position, and was entirely without influence or the acquaintance of persons of influence, but was resolved to perform my part in a struggle threatening the very existence of the nation. I performed a conscientious duty,

without asking for promotion or command, and without a revengeful feeling toward any section or individual.

Notwithstanding this, throughout the war, and from my candidacy for my present office in 1868 to the close of the last presidential campaign, I have been the subject of abuse and slander scarcely ever equaled in political history, which today I feel that I can afford to disregard in view of your verdict, which I gladly accept as my vindication.

Whether the slanders on Grant had scarcely ever been equaled might be argued by historians, but his electoral triumph in 1872 over the hapless Greeley would prove no permanent vindication. Much worse was soon to come. "American political annals," William Hesseltine wrote, "reveal no President who was happier in his Second Administration than in his first. Grant's second term served only to tarnish his reputation." There is as yet no vindication: the damage, as Hofstadter's curt dismissal demonstrates, was great, far greater still. It is a lugubrious irony that the fervent defenses and apologiae of Grant's modern defenders, all seeking to overturn such judgments, seem only to reinforce the received wisdom. It is not only that they attract renewed interest in the issue; they tend also to be so ferocious in their defenses, so single-minded and sometimes tendentious, that they rekindle the very suspicions they aim to stifle. The continuing reputation of the Grant administration was perfectly summed up in casual conversation with an educated American (not a historian) in 2003: "Teapot Dome—wasn't that one of Grant's?"

The reiteration of the introductory phrase "although personally honest"—which stands like a chamberlain welcoming guests into a room full of prosecutors with hard evidence—itself invites suspicion. If students of Grant's presidency are willing to grant its truth that Grant was indeed an honest man (most are), it raises nonetheless another sticky question: how could all these things have happened in so small a compass? Even if the scandals were not linked, should not an alert, aggressive chief executive, an American president, have taken strong and immediate steps to ensure that members of his administration knew they were being held, now, to a much higher standard? Should he not have been more aggressively vigilant? Should he not have been far more vocal, more energetic, more willing (for the sake of his administration's reputation and his own) to be, in his contemporary William Ewart Gladstone's phrase, a good butcher?

To such questions two answers are ordinarily returned. The first is that the climate of scandal, of fraud, of corruption was, well, a climate, not susceptible, in its pervasiveness, of amendment or cure. Like other postwar worlds of politics, culture, and society (Regency England, America in the Roaring Twenties), the Gilded Age was a period richly hospitable to material ambition and the ways it might be gratified. The second is that much of what is called political corruption was not corruption at all, but the means by which democratic governance sustains itself: political patronage was both underpinning and concomitant of a vigorous two-party system. For their loyalty, supporters were rewarded with good, sometimes lucrative, jobs. Sometimes they abused them. Not only this; the Civil War having been fought and won, and Reconstruction moving slowly, if tediously, toward an unhappy conclusion, party leaders were no longer conjoined in ideological crusades and missions; their aim now was to sustain themselves in power, and "spoils" (like placemen in eighteenth-century England) were the means by which to do it. Hence the emergence of the great senatorial power brokers like Roscoe Conkling and House Speaker James Blaine. As objective correlative: Hesseltine sees in the difference between architecture of the Federalist period—simple, austere, clean-limbed, and white— and the new buildings of the Grant era the distinction between the political cultures of the two periods. In the early years of the Republic ambitions were to be gratified by the attainment of reputation, reputation for honor, and by a posthumous fame. In the years from the end of the Civil War to the turn of another century, ambition was fed and slaked (but never satisfied) by money, possessions, and the power these conferred.

And here was Grant, at the political center of this culture, a sitting president almost none of whose life to date had remotely prepared him to address such issues as were precipitated in and by such a climate; a man who grappled to his heart, with hoops of steel, the friends of his early travails, to whom loyalty to friends was a cardinal virtue, who had a neurotic horror of personal confrontation, and who in his life anticipated Henry Stimson's apothegm by fifty years: the way to make a man trustworthy is to trust him.

A brisk rehearsal of the major scandals (the word is neither precise nor comprehensive, but it is the familiar label) of the Grant administration follows.

THE CREDIT MOBILIER

The best-known scandal of the Grant era had nothing to do with Ulysses Grant. It was the discovery of its elements, late in the presidential campaign of 1872, and the revelations soon produced, that served to link it in the public mind with the administration. "Credit Mobilier" was a dummy Pennsylvania corporation bought by the directors of the Union Pacific Railroad. They made themselves directors of the Credit Mobilier and used it as the primary construction company to build the railway. They paid themselves extravagantly, much of the funding coming from government subsidies, which were also used to pay subcontractors. This was in 1867. One of the principals, both a director of the company and a member of the House of Representatives, was Oakes Ames of Massachusetts, who, thinking to forestall adverse action by the Congress, when it discovered what was going on, passed out shares of Credit Mobilier stock to members of both the Senate and House. Some saw the shares for what they were—bribes—and refused them; others took them, claiming they were gifts; still others asked Ames to "hold them for me." Ultimately Ames and another congressman, James Brooks, were censured by the House; a third party was expelled from the Senate. Those congressmen who condemned Ames nonetheless were at pains to convince him of their personal solicitude for his predicament. In extenuation Ames argued that giving shares to congressmen was "the same thing as going into a business community and interesting the leading men by giving them shares. . . . A member of Congress has a right to own property in anything he chooses to invest in. . . . There is no difficulty in inducing men to look after their own property." For where your treasure is, there will your heart be also.

THE SANBORN CONTRACTS

Contemporaries puzzled over Ulysses Grant's relationship with his old Civil War nemesis Benjamin Butler, the incompetent general who had commanded the Army of the James. One theory was that Grant's hatred of Charles Sumner was so intense that he lost no opportunity to do things that could antagonize him, and Butler offered him opportunities to do so. Judge Hoar told the story of Grant's defense of a dubious appointment of a young protégé of Butler's, William A. Simmons, as collector of the port of Boston. Hoar and Grant were walking together, one night, in Lafayette Park. They passed Sumner's house. According to Hoar, Grant shook his fist at it and said, "I shall not withdraw the nomination. That man up there has abused me in a way which I have never suffered from any other man living!"

After the Black Friday debacle, George Boutwell's successor as Treasury secretary was William A. Richardson, who, like Butler, was from Lowell, Massachusetts. He had served satisfactorily under Boutwell as assistant secretary, but without distinction—and he had reissued several million greenbacks, an inflationary move which ran counter to Grant's own known convictions on the economy. In turn Richardson agreed on a contract with another Butler crony, the Bostonian John D. Sanborn, by which Sanborn would recover delinquent taxes owed the federal government, in exchange for half the proceeds. This was the old moiety principle, which had been repealed in 1872 but, because of a rider to another bill, was allowed to continue for this enterprise. Richardson made contracts to this effect with Sanborn, first when he was assistant secretary of the Treasury, later as secretary. Sanborn was to gather the names of those owing delinquent taxes, railroad companies, for example.

Under contracts with the department, Sanborn collected more than $400,000, of which he kept half, claiming more than two-thirds of this amount went in expenses. A House committee carefully examined the whole enterprise in 1874 and discovered that much of the money was fraudulently obtained, that there had been connivance between Treasury Department officials and Sanborn, and that much of the sum would have been collected by the Internal Revenue Department in any case. It reflected badly on Sanborn, who was dismissed, and Richardson, who was sustained in government but reassigned as a justice in the Court of Claims. Grant meantime had met with members of the House committee and had asked them not to submit a resolution stating no confidence in Richardson. Let me take care of it, he had asked.

No criminal culpability was proved. But Grant had lost a chance to make a strong and public statement: namely, by firing Richardson outright and using the occasion to put others in such positions on notice. Grant's defenders content themselves by asserting Grant's personal probity (which no one has ever doubted) and pointing out, again, his loyalty to those he had appointed.

THE BACK PAY GRAB

Near the end of its session in March 1873, Congress voted itself a 50 percent pay raise—from $5,000 to $7,500 a year—and sharply increased the salaries of senior administration officials, justices of the Supreme Court, and the president himself. Grant's compensation was to be raised from $25,000 to $50,000. The bill passed easily, members of neither party alert to the outcry one of the bill's provisions seemed bound to provoke: namely, that the raise be made retroactive to the beginning of the Forty-second Congress two years earlier. Each member was therefore to realize a bonus equal to a full year's salary. Since the measure was part of the general appropriation bill for the new year, and passed on the last day of the congressional session, the president was obliged either to sign it or to call the new Forty-third Congress into an immediate special session to consider repeal of the offending provision. He signed the bill.

There had been no increase in legislators' compensation for more than twenty years, and such increases were surely appropriate for the president, vice president, cabinet, and justices. (The president, for example, was expected to absorb all expenses incidental to his running of the White House out of his private funds.) But the back pay provision shocked and infuriated the country. The outrage was generalized and not partisan. The measure was repealed by the Forty-third Congress that fall (though Grant's salary remained at the new level), and no Congress thereafter dared raise its compensation until the turn of the century. But though Democrats and Republicans both had supported the back pay "grab," the tincture of unseemly grasping after money, of courting private gain while in public service, and in a time of economic uncertainty, was deepest on the Grant administration and, invariably, on the president himself. He had done nothing wrong; but he had responded passively, accepting the bill as a fait accompli when he could and should have made it an issue.

THE INDIAN TRADING SCANDAL

A recent historian adduces the Belknap bribery scheme as the single example of real corruption charged to a major Grant appointee. William Belknap succeeded Grant's friend John Rawlins as secretary of war in October 1869. His wife got him to give the lucrative post-tradership at Fort Sill, Oklahoma, to her friend Caleb Marsh of New York City. Unfortunately for Marsh, the current trader was happy where he was. They worked out a deal: John S. Evans, the incumbent, could keep his job, but he would have to pay Marsh twelve thousand dollars per year, and Marsh agreed to give Mrs. Belknap six thousand dollars of this extorted amount.

Mrs. Belknap inconveniently died a year later, but the magnanimous Marsh made payments to one of the Belknap children and then to Mrs. Belknap's sister, who married the secretary herself! Later Marsh testified that Belknap knew very well what was going on because he had actually delivered some of the payments to him.

On March 1, 1876, the House Committee on Expenditures in the War Department met Belknap's counsel; that night they deliberated again. Belknap, moving preemptively to beat what he inferred would be an impeachment, hurried to the White House and tendered his resignation, in person, to President Grant, and Grant accepted it—acknowledging in writing that he had received the resignation with "great regret," and noting that it had been accompanied by Belknap's request that it be accepted at once. Meantime the president had met at breakfast with Treasury Secretary Benjamin Bristow, an avid and incorruptible administrator who had succeeded William Richardson, and Bristow, it can be assumed, briefed Grant on the charges to be made in an impeachment of Belknap.

Belknap's resignation having been accepted by the president, he could not be tried in the Senate, though the House impeached him the same afternoon. Late that summer, a Senate trial acquitted him; Roscoe Conkling and a majority were in agreement that private individuals could not be tried—and Belknap had resigned before the proceeding began.

It is not known why the president, at the moment of Belknap's appearance at the White House, on hearing the secretary's request, was not put on his guard; why he did not, at least, invite his guest to join him for a private conversation: please tell me, what circumstance impels this sudden act? Either Belknap would have told the truth, refused to be put to the question, or invented an excuse on the spur of the moment. In any case, Grant would have, should have, pressed the point. He did not. Rather than force a scene with a colleague whom he knew well, and liked, Grant shrugged, telling himself that at least the man was resigning and would be out of the way.

THE WHISKEY RING

For many years Treasury Department revenue agents connived with distillers for bribes to falsify the quantities of liquor being manufactured and distributed. It was easy enough to do and to get away with. Distillers would falsify amounts prepared for shipment, or agents might produce the necessary stamps for the amounts far in excess of what was manufactured and shipped. An 1874 estimate put the taxes dodged by distillers at between twelve and fifteen million dollars per year.

This figure was calculated by Treasury Secretary Bristow, who was soon rewarded with the most helpful resource of all, an unsolicited letter from the publisher of a St. Louis newspaper, who provided him the name of a journalist, Myron Colony, who had all the information necessary to break the ring and enable the convictions of its participants. Bristow made Colony an agent of the Treasury Department at once.

A coruscating, widening swirl of evidence began to identify participants great and small. Among the great was General John A. McDonald of St. Louis—the midwestern district revenue supervisor—whom Grant had appointed in 1870 on the warm advice of Orville Babcock. By April 1875 McDonald had confessed to his principal role in the ring, reminding Secretary Bristow, and, later, Bristow's aide Bluford Wilson, of his importance to the Republican party and its need for strong allies in the West.

Bristow informed the president of McDonald's culpability, it appears, and Wilson later intimated that Grant had urged "prosecution unimpeded by favoritism." The mass arrests went down, all over the country, on May 13, 1875. Bristow now told Grant that McDonald was the ringleader of the operation; two months later, visiting Grant in Long Branch, New Jersey, he told him that his aide Babcock was also deeply involved. Grant instructed Bristow, in writing, to ensure that "no guilty man escape if it can be avoided. Be especially vigilant . . . against all those who insinuate that they have high influence to protect, or to protect them." In August Bristow discovered a telegram sent to McDonald, its order in Babcock's handwriting but the message mysteriously signed "Sylph." It had been sent in December 1874, just as investigators were leaving Washington to examine McDonald's files. Babcock admitted authorship but claimed that the message—"I succeeded they will not go. I will write you"—had nothing to do with McDonald or the whiskey investigation. There were other telegrams, one of which, Grant's former aide Horace Porter later told investigators, was part of an effort to keep a woman quiet—a woman with whom the president had allegedly had an affair. There was no evidence to support such a claim; but, as a means of deflecting Bristow's invigilation, it seems a not very imaginative ploy.

By November, trials of the principals having begun, Babcock himself, hoping to avoid any kind of civil proceeding, asked the president to authorize a military court of inquiry. This was denied, and Babcock was tried in St. Louis, in a civil court, in February 1876.

The court exonerated Babcock, but his reputation had been soiled irretrievably, and the president had to let him go. He did so slowly and lightly, separating him from his White House duties while allowing him to retain his position as superintendent of buildings and grounds for Washington.

Bristow, sea-green incorruptible and blameless in all ways save for an intense and obvious desire to be the Republican nominee for president in 1876, resigned under pressure. The pressure had been applied directly by the president, who had come to believe that he himself was Bristow's main target, just as he had come to believe in Babcock's innocence. He wrote to Fish that Bristow was a man of "intense selfishness and ambition and . . . extreme jealousy and suspicions."

Such scandals, if that is their proper characterization, stud the years of the Grant administrations. Along with *alcohol* and *butchery, scandal* has remained the hardiest of labels for Ulysses Grant. All due allowances being made for the influence of "the times," of the pervasive corruption of government at all levels and both parties, and for the absence of any proof that Grant was personally culpable in any of these episodes, there remains an unavoidable impression of a certain moral obtuseness in Grant: a solipsism. This is the way I am, those who work with me must be as loyal to me as I am to them, and they must be as immune to the attractions of money, ill-gotten money, as I am. The pattern, reinforced by many cases not presented here, is plain enough: What I am hearing about this person is scurrilous. He may have made mistakes, but he is not dishonest. I will let him go only with the greatest regret, because that is what mere trading politicians do, and I will cushion his fall in any way I can. As for confronting an alleged miscreant among my close advisers, or addressing a large number of senior members of administration simply to put them on notice that I will not tolerate any deviation from the expectations of honorable conduct of the people's business, that would be to insult their characters and threaten our common loyalty.

The last man to leave the battlefield at Belmont and the only man not to flinch while sitting his horse in direct view of enemy soldiers was the same man who could not say no to a friend, and not even a very good friend at that.

13

A Noble Exit

From the autumn of 1873 until the end of Grant's second term, the nation was plunged into a full-blown financial panic and, consequently, a deep depression from which it was not to recover for five or six years. Its effects on the federal withdrawal from the South can scarcely be exaggerated. The triggering event was the failure of Jay Cooke's banking house: unable to sell its bonds for the financing of the Northern Pacific Railroad, it simply ceased operating. Over the next two years eighteen thousand businesses failed; a quarter of the country's railroads went under; unemployment touched 14 percent. Any active sympathy convertible into political support for Reconstruction was soon drained away.

In January 1874, the *New York Herald* argued that "Reconstruction, the carpet-baggers, the usurpation of power supported by troops—all this is dead weight . . . that if not speedily disengaged will carry republicanism to the bottom." Grant responded with an exasperation bordering on sarcasm: "I begin to think it is time for the Republican Party to unload . . . let Louisiana take care of herself, as Texas will have to do. I don't want any quarrel about Mississippi state matters referred to me. This nourishing of Monstrosities has nearly exhausted the life of the party." And in 1875, turning down a request for federal intervention from the governor of Mississippi, Adelbert Ames (a Massachusetts man and the son-in-law of Benjamin Butler), he let slip the unfortunate if accurate characterization of what had become the northern attitude toward Reconstruction: "The whole public are tired out with these autumnal outbreaks in the South." He had privately assured Butler that Ames could still count on him to do his duty to see the laws were faithfully executed; but Edwards Pierrepont, now attorney general, altered the message finally sent to the governor. Pierrepont stressed that only with the greatest reluctance, only after all other means had been exhausted, Mississippi Republicans showing themselves "the courage and the manhood to fight for their rights and to destroy the bloody ruffians," could a call for help be considered.

The president also came under enormous pressure to inflate the currency—the certain panacea, it was argued, for the crisis. From all sides, farmers and westerners who were allies of the president's particularly, came the demand to reissue greenbacks, perhaps as much as $100 million worth. Congress sent such a bill for the president's signature in April 1874, in the comfortable expectation that he would sign it. He had to. The cabinet was overwhelmingly for the legislation; the political consequences of a veto were incalculable.

John Russell Young, in *Around the World with General Grant*, recorded the president's reflections on what he did.

> The only time I ever deliberately resolved to do an expedient thing for party reasons, against my own judgment, was on the occasion of the inflation bill. I was never so pressed in my life to do anything as to sign that bill—never. It was represented to me that a veto would destroy the Republican Party in the West. . . . I resolved to write a message to show that the bill need not mean inflation. . . . I wrote the message with great care and put in every argument I could call up to show that the bill was harmless. When I finished my wonderful message, I read it over and said to myself, "What is the good of all this? You do not believe it. I know it is not true." . . . I resolved to do what I believed to be right, veto the bill!

The veto was sustained, and the Senate soon sent Grant a bill for the resumption of specie payments, the Specie Resumption Act.

Grant said at the time, "I believe it is in the power of Congress . . . to devise such legislation as will renew confidence, revive all the industries, start us on a career of prosperity to last many years, and to save the credit of the nation and the people."

Perhaps no single act of the Grant presidency better represents how the president thought and acted. All the familiar elements are present: distended silences while the president listens to arguments of cabinet members and others, betraying no hint as to his thinking; a profoundly conservative sense as to what the economy needs for the long haul—something stable and solid; and then acting directly on the dictates of conscience. And afterward, he had very little to say—except, years later, in a conversation with Young.

This having been said, the effect of the Panic of 1873 and the following long depression on the North's flagging interest in Reconstruction was severe, among the final death knells to what had been nobly conceived by the man Grant admired above all others. Lincoln had called Reconstruction "the greatest question ever presented to practical statesmanship." It was not then, nor has it ever been, answered frankly.

The final blow truly came in the congressional elections of 1874, a defeat for Grant's party that was among the most severe in American history. The depression and continuing exasperation with Reconstruction had prompted a huge voter turnout, transforming what had been a decisive Republican majority of 194–92 in the House into a 181–107 Democratic majority. A Republican initiative to increase election turnout in southern states through a new civil rights bill accomplished little, when passed in the lame-duck session of 1875. The bill lacked teeth; a provision for the integration of public schools was withdrawn, and the public venues in which the act made integration the law were mostly venues in which few blacks would ever venture. Nor was there any serious provision for enforcement.

In the summer of 1875, in response to an expression of enthusiastic support from the Pennsylvania Republican party for his renomination and election to a third term, Grant informed the Pennsylvanians and his cabinet that he would decline the nomination. He had had enough. His decision was firm.

As new presidential candidates began to emerge, it was obvious that as far as Reconstruction was concerned, "prudent" policies would be the building materials for their platforms. Those who advocated that southern governance be left exclusively in the hands of the "wise and thinking men" of the South would be most likely to attract delegates before and at the convention. In June 1876 the party selected Rutherford B. Hayes, the governor of Ohio, as its nominee—a safe, conventional, rather timorous choice. His opponent, chosen two weeks later, would be the Democratic reform governor of New York, Samuel J. Tilden. Neither man campaigned aggressively, and each was careful in his pronouncements on issues of Reconstruction and the South. Hayes promised to work for "the blessings of honest and capable self-government," which was understood as code for a disposition to withdraw bayonets from the South. Tilden committed himself to clean up corruption in Washington and lead the country out of economic depression.

South Carolina and Louisiana, two of the last unredeemed states, were holding state elections in October 1876. In each, Grant's intervention to ensure a relative absence of fraud and the protection of voters from the familiar activities of intimidators, and to uphold the results of the elections, would prove to be decisive. The situation in South Carolina was especially fraught, marked by a campaign of terror and intimidation led by former Confederate general Wade Hampton and by the murder of five black militiamen in Hamburg and the shooting of the town marshal. An ex-slave warned that the Republicans should be prepared to lose the presidential vote; Democrats would "wade in blood knee-deep." Grant responded to Governor Daniel Chamberlain's inevitable request for federal intervention by declaring a state of insurrection; the troops arrived, and the election went off quietly (if not wholly without evidence of fraud). In Louisiana Grant ordered General Sheridan to employ necessary force to ensure the protection of the state's returning board, the agency charged with authenticating ballots and guaranteeing that the results were legitimate. In an accompanying message to Chamberlain the president noted that in South Carolina the efforts to obstruct the political process had been "cruel, bloodthirsty, wanton, unprovoked . . . a repetition of the course that has been pursued in other Southern states in the past few years." Clearly he didn't want this to happen in Louisiana.

The early results of the presidential election on November 7 seemed to point to a Tilden victory. Hayes was losing the popular vote by more than 200,000, and, apparently, he was likely to lose the electoral count as well. By late on election night, Tilden's count stood at 184 (with 185 needed to elect), Hayes's at 166. But now three states' results were challenged by the Hayes camp: those of Louisiana, Florida, and South Carolina. Grant sensed that Tilden would likely be the winner, and he cautioned that a presidency fraudulently obtained must be prevented at all costs. "No man worthy of the office of President should be willing to hold it if counted or placed there by fraud." He warned General Sherman to prepare to put down possible violence in all three states and to keep military forces in Washington on the alert.

The electoral totals sent to Congress were in dispute, but the Constitution made no provision for the resolution of such an outcome. Grant, meeting Tilden's campaign chairman, Congressman Abram Hewitt, assured him that he would abide by the result whatever it turned out to be, and that he believed Tilden had probably won. The president suggested a joint committee of Congress as an adjudicating authority, and in mid-December Congress acted, authorizing a commission that comprised fifteen members: three Democrats and two Republicans from the House, three Republicans and two Democrats from the Senate, and five Supreme Court justices—two Democratic and two Republican appointees, with these four to select a fifth justice, the presumption being that they would appoint the independent David Davis, a former liberal Republican who had in fact opposed Grant's reelection. The bill did not pass the Senate easily, many Republicans voting against it. In the House two-thirds of the Republicans voted against, but it passed there as well.

A strange serendipity (for Republicans) now intervened. The Illinois legislature, unable to agree on a second term for Senator John Logan, appointed Justice Davis in his stead. The latter immediately declined his appointment to the electoral commission. The four justices now made another selection: the Republican Joseph Bradley.

All during February, an atmosphere of disquiet and real fear prevailed; would Tilden's supporters accept the result that (after Bradley's appointment) seemed likely to go against them? A series of informal negotiations among Hayes's and Tilden's congressional supporters followed. The handwriting was plain enough; Tilden had no chance of becoming president (he had distressed his backers by an unaccountably passive attitude toward the issue in any case), but the Democrats could offer serious obstructions to a successful Hayes presidency, particularly in its early days. On February 24 an informal caucus was held in a Washington hotel, comprising four southern Democrats and five Ohio supporters of Hayes. There was talk of assurance of federal subsidies to the South, for a railroad running to the Pacific; of a Republican commitment to southern representation in a Hayes cabinet. Most important was an understanding that federal troops would be withdrawn from the South soon after the inauguration and that the victories of Democratic gubernatorial candidates in Louisiana and South Carolina would be recognized. The historian Eric Foner notes that, whatever contemporaries may have believed about an explicit compact having been agreed on, "the terms of the 'Bargain of 1877' remain impossible to determine." Even so, he quotes the mordant irony of a southern freedman: "The whole South—every state in the South—has got [back] into the hands of the very men that held us as slaves."

The electoral count was not completed until February 28, four days before Inauguration Day. The commission, voting 8 to 7 along party lines, accepted certified Republican electoral slates from all three disputed states. This made the electoral count 185–184 in Hayes's favor, and the new president took the oath of office at the White House Saturday evening, March 3 (the date set for presidential inaugurations, March 4, falling that year on a Sunday). He had managed his success carefully and shrewdly, keeping well out of sight while the electoral crisis was being resolved. In his inaugural address, given at the public ceremony on Monday, March 5, he gave tongue to the platitudinous avowals that had helped things along—the South should have "wise, honest, and peaceful local self-government," but governments that "guard the interests of both races carefully and equally." He was the first of a quartet of presidents—along with James Garfield, Chester Arthur, and Benjamin Harrison—whom Thomas Wolfe memorably described as men of "gravely vacant and bewhiskered faces," men who now subsist in the common memory as interchangeable parts, like stuffed animals on a shelf in a toy store.

The next morning the Grants moved out of the White House.

Grant's performance of duty during the four months between the November election and Hayes's inauguration is surely among his finest hours. An American president is commander in chief, effective head of his political party, head of government, and head of state—all four. These roles are not wholly distinct; their intersections and assimilations are many and mutually dependent. Yet it is in the last of these, head of state, that Grant in this period was at his best and most useful. He represented in his firmness, dignity, disinterestedness, and independence those qualities most important to citizens in extended periods of national confusion and stress. A historian recently argued that by the end of the administration no one in the White House gave a damn for the black man. The evidence does not sustain such a verdict. Grant's hero Abraham Lincoln apart, blacks have never had a more constant or solicitous president than Ulysses Grant. He had moved a long distance from 1860, and his record is certainly not free of error, missteps, or misjudgments. But as president, Grant had surely fulfilled his commitment to those his service as a soldier had helped make free men and women.

14

The Final Chapter

Ten weeks after the inauguration of President Hayes, on May 17, 1877, Ulysses and Julia Grant, and young Jesse, sailed for Europe, intending a long and leisurely trip abroad. The Grants were happily restless as travelers, desiring not only to see strange lands and places but also, simply, to travel, to keep moving, to experience what they had not seen or known before. Their planned itinerary was rather vague; except for early fixtures in England, there was no set schedule. Grant had accumulated sufficient savings to underwrite a long trip, and while they were abroad, he would become the beneficiary of another large sum, a windfall from an investment in a mining company.

Others would join the party from time to time. One was Adolph Borie, Grant's Philadelphia friend and hapless secretary of the navy, and sometime chaperone of the Grants' daughter Julia. More important was John Russell Young, the *New York Herald* journalist assigned to accompany General and Mrs. Grant on their travels, and to send home columns about them. The trip would last two years and four months. Although he was usually treated and celebrated as a former head of state, it was as General Grant, not President Grant, that the world acclaimed him. The "undismayed survivor of a thousand receptions" now moved confidently and affably through numbing, ceaseless rounds of receptions, dinners, tours, levees, and reviews, but he seemed to thrive on them. Meantime, from the beginning of the journey on the *Indiana* the Grants had taken a delighted, almost sensuous pleasure in the enforced languor of ocean travel. Young reported that "the reticence which had characterized the manner of the ex-President during the many years of his onerous and toilsome employment in the service of his country, dropped from him as though it were a mask."

On arrival in England he was saluted as an American hero and champion of the interests of working-class people everywhere; as a man who had saved the American union and been the instrument in the ending of chattel slavery. He was viewed also as a kind of American everyman: as the incarnation of the great democracy's virtues and its ingratiating foibles. He met and was lionized by the fashionable, the political, the literary—and the royal, Queen Victoria included. He chatted with Thomas Hughes of *Tom Brown's School Days* and attended a reception at which the literary critic and poet Matthew Arnold was present; Arnold, unimpressed at the reception, would later become a great champion of *The Personal Memoirs of U. S. Grant.*

The public at home devoured Young's columns (later collected and tricked out with explanations and travel notes as *Around the World with General Grant*, in 1881). Readers enjoyed a vicarious engagement in the former first family's travels and encounters and could imagine themselves in situations similar, conducting themselves in the same way—with confident and unaffected American charm, the charm of the worthily naive.

The great trip took the Grants through Europe, the Middle East, India, China, Russia, and Japan. They met many of the great personages of the age (Queen Victoria, Otto von Bismarck, the emperor of China), and they moved tirelessly through galleries and museums, cathedrals, shrines and venues man-made and natural, some of which elicited novel, perhaps sly, judgments. Of Venice, for example, General Grant was reported to have said that it was a handsome city, except for the streets, which needed to be drained.

Everywhere, Grant charmed people by his unaffected simplicity. He often walked out unaccompanied, or with only a single companion. Alone he strode across the great courtyard of the German chancellery, flicking away his cigar as he entered the building for his visit with Prince Bismarck—then on break from long sessions with Benjamin Disraeli and Count Gorchakov at the famous Congress of Berlin, which had been convened to solve the intractable "Eastern Question." Young's dispatches captured many of Grant's conversations; they also recorded his recollections and judgments about the war, its generals, and leadership. Grant had an amused contempt for book learning in soldiers; such people, he said, "always knew what Frederick the Great did at one place, and Napoleon at another. Unfortunately for their plans, the rebels were always thinking of something else."

Toward the end of the trip Grant confided to his aide Adam Badeau that the thought of returning home filled him with dread, and that if there had been a ready means of getting from Japan to Australia he would have prolonged their stay in the Far East. The truth was that Grant was uncertain what to do with himself. He had no employment prospects; Galena held no appeal as a permanent residence; and he was both attracted and repelled by the thought that he was already, in the minds of the "Stalwart" wing of the Republican party, the best candidate for the party's presidential nomination the following summer. What they had read, and what they were hearing, was that Grant's national popularity was surging: as an American exemplar, revered and celebrated by people all over the world, he stood out plainly as the strongest candidate any party could nominate.

The Grants had been away a very long time—two years, four months—but they came home too soon. They were given a tumultuous welcome in San Francisco, traveled across the country in slow stages, even went on extended trips to Mexico and Cuba, the general idea being to keep Grant away from the political calculations and the depredations of rival pundits and politicians for as long as possible. Though "the old venom of attack had been dissipated by the disappearance of official power," so that Grant could once again be an authentic national hero, he had become a hero of a particular kind, one whose reputation transcended flaws and mistakes in judgment and failures as president. Back home, he became a present reminder of how things had gone wrong. And not even George Washington, it was everywhere argued, would consider serving beyond two terms. The truly noble do not answer the seductions of ordinary ambition.

Meantime the Republicans—Conkling, James D. Cameron, Logan particularly—played their hand as badly as possible, as bosses in the fell spirit of We Know Better. At the 1880 Republican convention in Chicago, Conkling insisted on the Unit Rule, requiring each state delegation to cast its entire bloc of ballots for a candidate who had merely achieved majorities. Grant had significant but by no means overwhelming majorities in New York, Illinois, and Pennsylvania. The convention rejected the Unit Rule, and delegates also rebuked Conkling for his attempt to expel three West Virginia delegates who would not endorse a party pledge to support the nominee, who-ever it would be.

After twenty-eight ballots the convention was deadlocked, the Grant forces holding at 307 votes, still shy of the 379 needed to nominate. The next day the roll call showed clearly the growth of an anti-Grant coalition, and the convention, on its thirty-sixth bal-lot, nominated James A. Garfield of Ohio, with 399 votes to Grant's final tally of 306.

It is plain that Grant wanted the nomination and sensed both the obstacles to achieving it and the enormous demands a third-term presidency would impose on him, should he be nominated and elected. The cliché is appropriate: he knew what he quietly sought was not in his best interest. He sought it anyway, but the Stalwart leaders into whose hands he had placed his fortunes botched the business crudely, needlessly alienating prospective sup-porters by their arrogant assumptions that they, not the delegates, knew what was best for the party.

In our time former presidents are able to sustain themselves com-fortably and appropriately after their terms of office. There are pen-sions, Secret Service details, offices, and staffs. There are memoirs to be sold and dictated (in that order, usually), addresses to be given at trade conventions and university commencements, board appointments, friends of means to be visited in warm places. Though their fellow citizens may honor a tradition of republican austerity, avowing particular admiration for the postpresidential careers of John Quincy Adams and Jimmy Carter, they are not uncomfortable with the idea of former presidents cashing in and living large.

There were no presidential pensions in the nineteenth century. The Grants had slender means upon their return from their trip: a farm, two small properties of Julia's, the income from two small trusts rich friends had established in their behalf—their combined yield about six thousand dollars a year. They had been given a comfortable town house on East Sixty-sixth Street in Manhattan, but they lacked the dedicated means to maintain it. Grant had to look for a job. After a significant false start, in which he briefly served, at nominal salary, as president of the Mexican Southern Railway (with offices on Wall Street), Grant gratefully accepted a sinecure as silent partner in the New York City investment firm of Grant and Ward— the principals were his son Ulysses Grant, Jr., and Ferdinand Ward, a rising star on Wall Street. The former president put $100,000 of his own money into the firm, certain that *gilt-edged*, as the firm was called by its friends, was a fair synonym for safe and profitable.

William McFeeley, a recent Grant biographer, crisply describes the business.

> Investors bought securities through the firm and . . . left them with [Grant and Ward] as collateral on loans with which they bought still more securities. Grant and Ward, then, in a perfectly legal and normal procedure, borrowed against the securities in order to invest for the firm's own account. What was not legal was in fact that Ferdinand Ward was rehypothecating the securities improperly by pledging the same stocks to support more than one bank loan.

On a Saturday in May 1884 Ward came to see Grant. He asked for $150,000 to help cover loans he had just made, to tide the firm over until the start of the workweek. To this date the firm had regularly paid dividends to its investors (as high, in one year, as 40 percent on principal). The loans now outstanding were in fact monies borrowed from the Marine Bank, whose president was another partner in Grant and Ward. Now the Marine Bank was itself in danger of collapse, according to Ward, because of demands made on the bank by the city of New York.

Grant went to William H. Vanderbilt, who made him a personal loan of $150,000. Grant gave this money to Ward. It was the last he ever saw of it; two days later the firm and the Marine Bank both crashed. Far from its listed capitalization of fifteen million dollars, Grant learned, the firm's total assets were less than sixty thousand dollars. Ward and his bank partner were soon tried, convicted of larceny and embezzlement, and given lengthy jail sentences. Grant was destitute.

Remembering Grant's reaction to the awful blow, Mark Twain described his astonishment at his composure and forbearance: "That countenance of his never betrayed him." (In the larger sense, of course, it had betrayed Grant all his life, obscuring and masking all evidences of passion, joy, anguish, grief. The suffering of the man he revered above all others, Abraham Lincoln, was palpable; it was, in the political calculus of democratic effectiveness, an asset.) For Grant the failure of the firm was devastating. Here, before the public, was shaming evidence of a pathetic credulity, of abject unfitness for the work of commercial business (the calling of so many successful men whom Grant admired), and of his son's stupidity. And now he and Julia were, literally, almost broke.

They scraped by. There were touching, unsought loans and gifts, one for five hundred dollars with this note appended: "General, I owe you this for Appomattox." Vanderbilt himself assumed title to the house, to protect it from creditors, allowing the Grants to live there until Julia's death, with the understanding that Grant's military memorabilia and library would be left to the nation. And not long afterward Grant told *Century* magazine (whose editors had approached him earlier about writing an article on the Civil War) that he had reconsidered the proposition and was prepared to submit articles on Shiloh and Vicksburg. He was offered five hundred dollars for the first of them.

Mark Twain had in fact earlier suggested that Grant try his hand
at writing, and this was not *Century*'s first proposal either. Grant set
to work on the essay on Shiloh (which the editor tactfully suggested needed more vivid, humanizing anecdotes) and, later, once
settled in Long Branch for the summer of 1884, a longer account of
Vicksburg.

In midsummer, Grant swallowed part of a peach and felt a sharp
and frightening pain at the back of his throat. The pain almost
unnerved him. After a while it grew dull; then it subsided, only to
recur as the summer progressed. Grant did what most strong men
do in such circumstances: nothing. Whether he guessed at what the
pain must portend, we cannot know; in any case there was no
known connection between cancer and smoking in 1884. But the
disease that was finally confirmed in October was certainly the consequence of a tobacco habit that had gripped Grant since his Mexican War days in the 1840s. In a thorough catalog of President Grant's
qualities of character and temperament, his habits of work (in
which spasms of concentrated industry seemed to alternate with
strange stretches of torpor), the crotchets and quirks of his personality and appearance, the historian Allan Nevins notes that "his one
vice, when he entered the White House, was tobacco. He reeked
with it; his cigars were black, rank, and poisonous; he consumed
them in huge quantities, even more than Edwin Booth."

The disease would defeat the available resources of Gilded Age
medicine. It would kill him, taking its time about it, occasionally
allowing weeks and even months of reprieve and renewed energy,
but moving inexorably to an end that was certain. The cancer was
the dark continuo in the final movement of a life that now became
most heroic when devoted to the most prosaic of labors, writing his
memoirs. It would be a long (275,000-word) description of what he
had learned and seen, about himself as well as about war, about leaders, friendship, and the peoples and places where he had fought—
devoted almost entirely to the war in Mexico and the Civil War.

The *Century* editors had proposed this more ambitious project,
offering a standard royalty and no advance. Mark Twain, whose counsel Grant sought, was outraged: *Century*'s proposal was one they

"would have offered to any unknown Comanche Indian whose book they thought might sell 3,000 or 4,000 copies." He made a counter-offer on behalf of his own publisher (Twain himself and his partner, Charles Webster), which Grant accepted only reluctantly, concerned that he had somehow incurred a moral obligation to *Century*. The arrangement, itself testimony to Grant's concern that Twain not suffer loss should the book fail, assigned 70 percent of the net profits from the book to the author.

By the late winter of 1885, Julia Grant and the family, and now the country, knew that Ulysses Grant was dying. How long he would live could only be guessed at. Already eating had become difficult, swallowing terribly painful. Mark Twain was shocked at his appearance. But Grant was fully committed to the book, working on it eight hours a day, helped out initially by Adam Badeau, who had already published his own military history of the war, and by his eldest son, Fred. He was meticulous in checking facts, scrupulous in his efforts to be fair in his appraisals of other men's abilities and motivations, and of their strengths or shortcomings as generals or politicians. Grant imprinted his will, his character, his understanding of the Mexican and Civil Wars on the narrative. Writing of other men's struggles, of their campaigns and their successes and failures, he did so in a way that presented a remarkable self-portrait: as a man of sterling common sense, unfailing chivalry, unguessed-at resources of humor and compassion both. Above all, Grant displays an unself-conscious willingness, unusual in soldiers of any stamp, to confide self-doubt. The following famous passage may be taken as typical; it is Grant's description of his response to Lee's surrender at Appomattox.

> Whatever [General Lee's] feelings, they were entirely concealed from my own observation; but my own feelings, which had been quite jubilant on the receipt of his letter, were sad and depressed. I felt like anything rather than rejoicing at the downfall of a foe who had fought so long and so valiantly, and had suffered so much for a cause, though that cause was, I believe, one of the worst for which a people ever fought.

Grant survives in the national consciousness partly as a force, as will, determination, imperturbability. When Edwin Stanton mistook Grant's medical director for the general, expecting a massive bearded figure, something like a German tribesman in a blue uniform, he was only repeating an error hundreds of men and women had made, and would make, during Grant's lifetime and afterward. He also survives, barely and dimly, as a shrunken figure in a wicker chair on an Adirondack veranda, swaddled in a black cloak and wearing what looks like a skullcap or a longshoreman's wintertime wool hat. He is perhaps writing, scratching away on a large pad propped up on his lap, probably revising or reading proofs of the *Memoirs*. He is only a week or two from death, but he is completing his duty to Julia and his family, knowing now that the book will be a success in the way that matters most—the only financial success he will ever have achieved, and the only one that can count: the one that will protect his family. He has written it thoroughly and told the exact truth and been as accurate as possible.

Very few visitors were allowed to say good-bye. Among them was Simon Bolivar Buckner, a friend from cadet days, from Mexico, from New York City (when Ulysses was destitute and needed the money to pay a hotel bill and get home), and from Fort Donelson and Unconditional Surrender. By then Grant could communicate only in whispers and in penciled notes. He let ministers and doctors poke at him—if you think it will do any good, I suppose it can't do any harm—and finally allowed himself to be put to bed. His suffering was very great and prolonged, but he bore it with the same composure he had borne all the other travails of his life. He died on July 23, 1885. He was sixty-three years old.

Milestones

1822 Hiram Ulysses Grant born in Point Pleasant, Ohio, on April 27

1839–43 Grant attends the United States Military Academy in West Point, New York, and is rechristened Ulysses Simpson Grant

1845 Annexation of Texas

1846 Mexico declares war on the United States; Grant sees first combat at Palo Alto, Resaca de la Palma, and Monterrey, under the command of General Zachary Taylor

1847 Capture of Mexico City by General Winfield Scott's troops

1848 Treaty of Guadalupe Hidalgo ends the Mexican War; Grant marries Julia Dent; Taylor elected president

1852 Grant assigned to peacetime military duty in California

1854 Grant resigns from the U.S. Army; Kansas-Nebraska Act passed; formation of the Republican party

1856 James Buchanan wins the presidency, defeating John C. Frémont, the first Republican presidential candidate

1857 Dred Scott decision

1858 Lincoln-Douglas debates

1860 Grant moves to Galena, Illinois; Abraham Lincoln elected president; secession crisis

1861 Lincoln takes office; Fort Sumter attacked and captured by Confederate troops; Grant appointed colonel of the Twenty-first Illinois volunteers regiment in June and is promoted to brigadier general two months later; wins Battle of Belmont on November 6

1862 Grant forces unconditional surrender of Fort Donelson on February 16; Battle of Shiloh, April 6–7

1863 Lincoln issues the Emancipation Proclamation; Battle of Gettysburg; surrender of Vicksburg; Union victory at Chattanooga

1864 Grant promoted to lieutenant general and commanding general, all Union armies; Battle of the Wilderness; fall of Atlanta; Sherman's "march to the sea"

1865 Grant receives Lee's surrender at Appomattox on April 9; assassination of Abraham Lincoln on April 14; ratification of Thirteenth Amendment, eliminating slavery

1868 Impeachment of President Andrew Johnson; ratification of the Fourteenth Amendment; Grant elected president

1869 Grant inaugurated on March 4; "Black Friday" scandal; Santo Domingo controversy

1870 Ratification of the Fifteenth Amendment, granting blacks the right to vote

1871 Last of the southern states, Georgia, to be reseated in Congress; Ku Klux Klan Act passed; Washington Treaty signed with Great Britain

1872 Grant reelected president

1873 "Back Pay Grab" by Congress; Panic of 1873 begins economic depression and crisis

1874 Veto of congressional greenback bill; Democrats regain control of House of Representatives in midterm elections

1875 Grant signs Specie Resumption Act; declares he will not seek a third term

1876–77 Disputed presidential election between Rutherford B. Hayes and Samuel J. Tilden; Hayes declared victor by electoral commission on February 28, 1877

1877–79 Grant and Julia take their round-the-world trip

1880 Grant's name placed in nomination at Republican convention, but effort fails; James A. Garfield nominated and elected president

1881 Assassination of Garfield; Chester Arthur becomes president

1884 Collapse of the Grant and Ward firm, ruining Grant financially

1885 Grant dies at Mt. McGregor, New York, on July 23; publication of Grant's *Memoirs* restores family finances

Selected Bibliography

Source materials available to scholars and students of Ulysses S. Grant comprise numerous manuscript collections, congressional reports, presidential messages.

The Personal Memoirs of U. S. Grant (Cambridge: Da Capo Press, 2001) are devoted almost entirely to a narrative history of the Mexican War and the Civil War, and of the author's role in each. Grant is a writer of rare fluency and accuracy: he is devastatingly honest in his judgments of himself, and not without a certain *gaminerie.*

Any serious student of U. S. Grant's career must rely principally on *The Papers of U. S. Grant,* volumes 1–26 (volume 26 ends in 1875; several more volumes are planned), edited by John Y. Simon (Carbondale: Southern Illinois University Press, 1967). Since 1962, Dr. Simon has supervised the collection and editing of all Grant personal papers. His is a monumental achievement.

Several biographies of Grant, studies of the Grant presidency, and books on politics, the economy, Reconstruction, and foreign policy have been particularly useful to my book:

Apart from one or two studies, William B. Hesseltine, *Ulysses Grant, Politician* (New York: Frederick Ungar, 1935), remains the only full-scale literal biographical consideration of Grant as president. The book is brilliant, exhaustive, quirky, and often funny. A snobbism—the condescension of the brilliant scholar to the rude and taciturn politician—inflects the text throughout.

William McFeeley, *Grant* (New York: Norton, 1982), covers the full life of Grant. Much praised on publication, it is uneven in quality and often hostile to Grant, and particularly critical of Grant's presidential leadership during Reconstruction. The book is full of clever imputation, most of it amusing, some of it wrong.

Geoffrey R. Perret, *Ulysses S. Grant: Soldier and President* (New York: Random House, 1997), is a strong, rambunctious biography, strongly prejudiced *in* Grant's favor.

John A. Carpenter, *Ulysses S. Grant* (New York: Twayne, 1970), is the best available small biography of Ulysses S. Grant. It is careful, judicious, meticulously researched, and fair. The book focuses mainly on the Grant presidency.

Brooks D. Simpson, *Ulysses S. Grant, Triumph Over Adversity, 1822–1865* (New York: Houghton Mifflin, 2000), is the first volume of a projected two-volume biography of Grant. A meticulous scholar, Simpson has devoted most of his professional life to a consideration of Grant's role in the Civil War, and, particularly, during the period between Grant's victory, in 1865, over Lee and his election to the presidency in 1868.

Frank J. Scaturro, *President Grant Reconsidered* (New York: Madison Books, 1999), examines the Grant presidency, focusing particularly on Reconstruction. Scaturro, like Brooks Simpson, communicates a sympathetic understanding for his subject; the book notably considers the *sources* of anti-Grant bias in earlier biographies and monographs.

Jean Edward Smith, *Grant* (New York: Simon and Schuster, 2001), is the definitive one-volume life of U. S. Grant: full of detail, comprehensive, and scrupulously fair. Like McFeeley, Smith does not stint on detailed consideration of relatively obscure aspects of Grant's career.

Two other useful biographies are Louis A. Coolidge, *Ulysses S. Grant* (New York: Houghton Mifflin, 1917), and Hamlin Garland, *Ulysses S. Grant: His Life and Character.* 2nd edition (New York: Macmillan, 1920).

Julia D. Grant, in *The Personal Memoirs of Julia Dent Grant*, edited by John Y. Simon (Carbondale: Southern Illinois University Press, 1975), looks back on her life with U. S. Grant.

Another helpful memoir is John Russell Young, *Around the World with General Grant* (Baltimore: Johns Hopkins University Press, 2002). Much of this engaging book, written by a young *New York Herald* reporter, comprises long reminiscences—principally of men and battles—that Grant communicated to Young on shipboard. Here particularly are to be found Grant's judgments of Confederate generals and generalship.

GENERAL HISTORIES, MONOGRAPHS, AND ARTICLES

Ackerman, Kenneth D. *Dark Horse: The Surprise Election and Political Murder of James A. Garfield.* New York: Carol and Graf, 2003.
Ambrose, Stephen. *To America.* New York: Simon and Schuster, 2002.

Boutwell, George S. "General Grant's Adminstration: From the Standpoint of a Member of His Cabinet."

Carpenter, John A. "Washington, Pennsylvania, and the Gold Conspiracy of 1869." *Western Pennsylvania Historical Magazine*, 1965.

Catton, Bruce. *Grant Takes Command*. Edison, N.J.: Castle Books, 2000.

———. *This Hallowed Ground*. Edison, N.J.: Castle Books, 2002.

———. *U. S. Grant and the American Military Tradition*. New York: Grosset and Dunlap, 1954.

Coolidge, Louis A. *American Statesmen, Second Series: Ulysses S. Grant*. New York: Houghton Mifflin, 1917.

Crane, James L. "Conversations Between Grant and His Chaplain." Ulysses S. Grant Association Web page, 2002.

Donald, David Herbert. *Lincoln*. New York: Simon and Schuster, 1995.

Donald, David Herbert, Jean Harvey Baker, and Michael F. Holt. *The Civil War and Reconstruction*. New York: Norton, 2001.

Feis, William B. *Grant's Secret Service*. Lincoln, Neb.: University of Nebraska Press, 2002.

Foner, Eric. *Reconstruction: America's Unfinished Revolution, 1863–1877*. New York: Harper and Row, 1988.

Foote, Shelby. *The Civil War: A Narrative*. New York: Random House, 1958.

Freehling, William W. *The Road to Disunion*. New York: Oxford University Press, 1990.

Fuller, Major General J. F. C. *Grant and Lee: A Study in Personality and Generalship*. Bloomington: Indiana University Press, 1957.

Gillette, William. "Election of 1872." In A. M. Schlesinger Jr., ed., *History of American Presidential Elections 1789–1968*. New York: McGraw-Hill, 1971.

———. *Retreat from Reconstruction, 1869–1879*. Baton Rouge: Louisiana State University Press, 1979.

Good, Warden. "American Finance, 1860–1880." Unpublished paper, 2002.

Gould, Lewis L. *Grand Old Party*. New York: Random House, 2003.

Grant, Ulysses S. "First Inaugural Address." March 4, 1869.

———. "Second Inaugural Address." March 4, 1873.

Hofstadter, Richard. *The American Political Tradition and the Men Who Made It*. New York: Vintage Books, 1989.

Hoogenboom, Ari. *Outlawing the Spoils: A History of the Civil Service Reform Movement, 1865–1883*. Chicago: University of Illinois Press, 1961.

———. *Rutherford B. Hayes: Warrior and President*. Kansas: University of Kansas Press, 1995.

Hughes, Nathaniel Cheairs. *The Battle of Belmont: Grant Strikes South*. Chapel Hill: University of North Carolina Press, 1991.

Israel, Fred L., ed. *The State of the Union Messages of the Presidents, 1790–1966*. New York: Chelsea House, 1967.

Lewis, Lloyd. *Captain Sam Grant*. Boston: Little, Brown, 1950.

Lorant, Stephan. *The Presidency*. New York: Macmillan, 1951.

McPherson, James M. *Battle Cry of Freedom: The Civil War Era*. New York: Ballantine Books, 1988.

———. *Ordeal by Fire: The Civil War and Reconstruction*. 3rd ed. New York: McGraw-Hill, 2001.

McWhiney, Grady, ed. *Grant, Lee, Lincoln and the Radicals*. Baton Rouge: Louisiana State University Press, 2001.

Morgan, H. Wayne. *The Gilded Age: A Reappraisal*. Syracuse: Syracuse University Press, 1963.

Morrison, James L., Jr. *The Best School in the World*. Kent: Kent State University Press, 1986.

Mundy, Erik S. *The Ambiguity of the National Idea: The Presidential Campaign of 1872*. Charlottetown: University of Prince Edward Island, 1978.

Nevins, Allan. *Hamilton Fish: The Inner History of the Grant Administration*. New York: Frederick Ungar, 1967.

Porter, Horace. *Campaigning with Grant*. New York: Konecky and Konecky, 1999.

Rhea, Gordon C. *Cold Harbor*. Baton Rouge: Louisiana State University Press, 2002.

Roseboom, Eugene, and Francis Weisenburger. *A History of Ohio*. New York: Prentice-Hall, 1934.

Rossiter, Clinton. "The Presidents and the Presidency." *American Heritage*, April 1956.

Sefton, James E. *The United States Army and Reconstruction, 1865–1877*. Baton Rouge: Louisiana State University Press, 1967.

Simon, John. "Ulysses S. Grant One Hundred Years Later." *Illinois Historical Journal*, vol. 79 (1986).

Simpson, Brooks D. *Let Us Have Peace: Ulysses S. Grant and the Politics of War and Reconstruction, 1861–1868*. Chapel Hill: University of North Carolina Press, 1991.

———. *The Reconstruction Presidents*. Kansas: University Press of Kansas, 1998.

Trefousse, Hans L. *Andrew Johnson*. New York: Norton, 1989.

Weigley, Russell F. *History of the United States Army*. New York: Macmillan, 1967.

White, Ronald C., Jr. *Lincoln's Greatest Speech: The Second Inaugural*. New York: Simon and Schuster, 2002.

Wilson, Edmund. *Patriotic Gore: Studies in the Literature of the American Civil War*. New York: Oxford University Press, 1962.

Winik, Jay. *April 1865: The Month That Saved America.* New York: HarperCollins, 2001.

Woodward, C. Vann. "The Lowest Ebb." *American Heritage,* vol. 8, no. 3 (1957), pp. 53–108.

———, ed. *Responses of the Presidents to Charges of Misconduct.* New Haven, Conn.: Dell, 1974.

Acknowledgments

I owe particular debts of gratitude to several friends and colleagues who were generous with time and counsel in my preparation of this small book on Ulysses Grant: John Y. Simon, dean of Grant historiography—as wise, judicious, shrewd, and self-effacing as his subject—was particularly helpful. Two other Grant scholars, Brooks Simpson and Jean Edward Smith, provided valuable advice and aperçus. Former secretary of the army John O. Marsh was most helpful in the early stages of my research.

I also want to thank Selma Brittingham, David McCullough—who is unfailingly generous to anyone who writes history or biography, however small their pretensions to do either—Lori O. Parrent, Gardner Mundy, Kevin Rolando, Fitzgerald Bemiss, Waite Rawles, Joseph J. Ellis, Professor James Robertson, Professor Spencer Tucker, Generals Montgomery Meigs and Casey Brower, Ward Good, Jack Chambliss, Colonel Cash Koeniger, Victor Davis Hanson, John Winslow, Louise Grosvenor, Patrick Lang, Kenneth Cribb. Finally, I must thank my editor at Times Books, Paul Golob; the general editor of the American Presidents series and an inspiration to all American historians, Arthur Schlesinger, Jr.; my agent, Tina Bennett; and my wife, Diana Bunting.

Index

ABOUT THE AUTHOR

JOSIAH BUNTING III is a former army officer who for eight years led his alma mater, the Virginia Military Institute. His earlier books include *The Lionheads, The Advent of Frederick Giles, An Education for Our Time,* and *All Loves Excelling.* He serves currently as chairman of the National Civic Literacy Board at the Intercollegiate Studies Institute in Wilmington, Delaware. He lives with his family in Newport, Rhode Island.